WITHDRAWN

THE
BUDDHIST POETRY
of the
GREAT KAMO PRIESTESS

Michigan Monograph Series in Japanese Studies
Number 5

Center for Japanese Studies
The University of Michigan

THE BUDDHIST POETRY *of the* GREAT KAMO PRIESTESS

Daisaiin Senshi and *Hosshin Wakashū*

by

EDWARD KAMENS

ANN ARBOR

Center for Japanese Studies
The University of Michigan

1990

© 1990

by

Center for Japanese Studies
The University of Michigan
108 Lane Hall
Ann Arbor, MI 48109–1290

Library of Congress Cataloging-in-Publication Data

Kamens, Edward, 1952-
  The Buddhist poetry of the Great Kamo Priestess : Daisaiin Senshi and Hosshin wakashū / by Edward Kamens.
      p. cm. — (Michigan monograph series in Japanese studies : no. 5)
  Includes the text of Hosshin wakashū.
  Includes bibliographical references.
  ISBN 0-939512-41-6
  1. Senshi, Princess, daughter of Murakami, Emperor of Japan, 964–1035. Hosshin wakashū. 2. Buddhism in literature. I. Senshi, Princess, daughter of Murakami, Emperor of Japan, 964-1035. Hosshin wakashū. 1990. II. University of Michigan. Center for Japanese Studies. III. Title. IV. Series.
PL789.S43H635 1990
895.6′114—dc20   89-71219
                                                                                                              CIP

A Note on the Type

This book is typeset in Palatino. This face, designed by Hermann Zapf, combines a distinctly modern flavor with a calligraphic influence of its 16th-century heritage.

Composed by Typographic Insight, Ltd., Ann Arbor, Michigan
Index by AEIOU Inc.
Printed and bound by Braun-Brumfield, Inc., Ann Arbor, Michigan
Book design by Marty Somberg

∞

The paper used in this publication meets the requirements of the ANSI Standard Z39.48-1984 (Permanence of Paper).

This book is dedicated to the memory of

Carolyn Wheelwright

1939–1989

CONTENTS

ACKNOWLEDGMENTS

Support for this study was received from the Northeast Asia Council of the Association for Asian Studies, Inc., the Enders Fund of the Yale University Graduate School, and the Council on East Asian Studies of Yale University. Kadokawa Shoten graciously permitted reproduction of the text of *Hosshin wakashū* from volume 3 (*Shikashū hen* I) of the *Shinpen kokka taikan*. I wish to thank Professor Hashimoto Yuri and Professor Ishihara Kiyoshi for discussing Senshi and her poetry with me; Professor Stanley Weinstein and Richard Jaffe, for their assistance with questions of religious history and thought; and Professor Robert N. Huey, for a very close examination of one of the final drafts of this book and innumerable suggestions for its improvement. Mary Miller has helped and encouraged me all along the way: I cannot thank her enough.

ABBREVIATIONS

HSWKS   *Hosshin wakashū*

NKBT   *Nihon koten bungaku taikei.* 100 vols. Tokyo: Iwanami Shoten, 1957–69.

SKT   *Shinpen kokka taikan* Henshū Iinkai, ed. *Shinpen kokka taikan.* Tokyo: Kadokawa Shoten, 1983–.

T   Takakusu Junjirō and Watanabe Kaigyoku, eds. *Taishō shinshū daizōkyō.* 85 vols. Tokyo: Taishō Issaikyō Kankōkai, 1924–32.

Zakki   *Kamo chūshin zakki*

PROLOGUE

This is a study of ways of reading some Japanese poems (*waka*) written by the woman known as "the Imperial Princess Senshi" (*Senshi Naishinnō*) or as "the Great Kamo Priestess Senshi" (*Daisaiin Senshi*, or simply *Daisaiin*). She was born in 964 and died in 1035, in the Heian period of Japanese history (794–1185). Most of the poems discussed here are what may loosely be called Buddhist poems, since they deal with Buddhist scriptures, practices, and ideas. For this reason, most of them have been treated as examples of a category or subgenre of *waka* called *Shakkyōka*, "Buddhist poems," or more literally, "poems on, about, or relating to the teachings and practices of Buddhism." In this term, *Shakkyō* means "Buddha's (i.e., Śākyamuni's) teachings," although the teachings referred to are by no means limited to those of the "historical Buddha," and *ka* means poem here as it does in *waka*, a Sino-Japanese word for "Japanese poem" as distinguished from *shi* or *kanshi*, "Chinese poem."

The very use of the term "Buddhist poems," *Shakkyōka*, in reference to Senshi's poems suggests a certain way of reading those poems. But one of the things this study will show is that such a reading, if too encumbered by notions about that classification or genre, may mask the very important fact that most of her poems (and many others so classified) are really more like other poems in the *waka* canon than they are unlike them. In the case of Senshi's "Buddhist poems," especially the ones examined closely here, the links, through language, to the traditions of secular verse are explicit, and are very much in keeping with the expressed purpose of her project, which was to use the essentially secular and public literary language of *waka*, of which she had considerable and widely acknowledged mastery, to address and express very serious and relatively private religious concerns and aspirations. In reading Senshi's poems, it is as important to think about their relationship to the traditions and conventions of *waka* and to other *waka* texts as it is to think about their relationship to Buddhist thought, practices, and texts.

Some of Senshi's poems discussed here may be encountered in more than one context in the canons of Japanese poetry. The effect of reading these poems in the context of her so-called "private collections" (*shikashū*), which actually contain poems not only by Senshi but also by women of her "salon" or retinue, or in the context of the cycle entitled *Hosshin wakashū* ("A Collection of Japanese Poems for the Awakening of Faith"[1]),

---

1. Hereafter this work will be cited in notes as *HSWKS*.

which will receive special attention in this study, is very different from their effect when they are read grouped with others judged to be "of their kind," in one sense or another, by the compilers of the canonical *waka* anthologies (*chokusenshū*, i.e., imperially commissioned collections of Japanese poetry). *Waka* studies both in Japan and elsewhere tend to focus almost exclusively on the major *waka* anthologies—the *Kokin wakashū*, the *Shin kokin wakashū*, and the like—and for good reason, given their historical importance and the masterful effects achieved therein through the sophisticated arrangement of poems culled from diverse sources. The circumstances in which these anthologies were created imparted great prestige to them, and that prestige was imparted in turn to their contents. As a result, these anthologies have been dominant among the various settings in which readers have, for centuries, encountered the works of Japanese poets. But many of the poems encountered in such settings also can be and should be read within their original or at any rate alternative contexts: in cycles of poems composed for inscription on commemorative works of art, or in the competitive and highly charged sociopolitical setting of the *utaawase*, or poetry contest; or as self-contained entities conceived and composed for sharing in more intimate circumstances, such as those that appear to have pertained in the composition of *Hosshin wakashū*. When read in such contexts, new things come to light in these poems, things that may be obscured in the anthologized contexts, intriguing and appealing though they may be. By returning as best we can to contexts that we may think of as closer to those in which the poems were first conceived, composed, and read, we may also regain a sense of immediacy between poet and poem.

One finds, however, that if the reading context in which one encounters almost any traditional Japanese poem is a traditional Japanese context—be it an anthology (for example, a *chokusenshū* or *shikashū*), a narrative (for example, one of the many kinds of *monogatari* or *nikki*, i.e., "tales" or "diaries," categories that often overlap), or a theatrical script (such as the text of a Nō play) that makes extensive use of or reference to poems—one must inevitably come to terms with contextualizing information therein presented, in one way or another, concerning the poet and the circumstances in which he or she wrote that poem. Such information is presented in many traditional texts to their readers as "fact" or "history" in order to shape the way those readers read those texts—as happens, for example, with *kotobagaki*, the prose lead-ins supplied by traditional anthology editors to tell as much as can credibly be told (and sometimes more) about how poems got written, by whom, and in what circumstances.

Analysis of the dynamics of such contextualized readings, which are shaped by the interests and aims of writers other than those who wrote the poems, is a multifaceted problem that is addressed in various ways in this study. In particular, however, it is addressed here in reference to the ways that Senshi's poems have been read both in the past and in recent times. Given what others have done, it is not always easy to read Senshi's poems first, and let them take precedence, before interpreting them, as is the custom, in light of what is known or supposed (often on the basis of the poems themselves) about the poet. Even in this study, Senshi's poems are not read or treated as groups of signifiers adrift in a void but as utterable texts consciously crafted at a specific time by a specific person. It is not possible to retrieve a complete sense or understanding of the conditions of that time and the circumstances in which that person acted, and it is dangerous to try to reconstruct that time and those circumstances from the products thereof (the texts of the poems) alone. This study, therefore, also creates a context for the reading of Senshi's poems by presenting what is known and what has been thought about her and them beforehand, but it does so to show, among other things, that the reading contexts created through such presentations produce only one or some of the many possible readings of those poems. In my reading, Senshi remains present as a historical personality, for it is my belief that poems get written in certain ways by the people who write them because of certain things about those people and the conditions and contexts in which they write—but one must be aware of how one comes by one's knowledge of such things and of how it affects one's reading. The historical Senshi, however one knows or perceives her, is, at any rate, not completely identical with the persona or personae that "speak" in her poems, and, furthermore, what one does or does not know about her does not necessarily decree what any one of her poems may or may not mean in one context or another or to one reader or another.

The single piece of information that has played the greatest role in shaping readings of Senshi's poems, both in the past and recently, is the seemingly anomalous fact that she wrote "Buddhist poems," and through them expressed something of her Buddhist faith, while she was at the same time High Priestess of the Kamo Shrines (*Saiin*)—that is, an imperially appointed official of the indigenous religious tradition called "Shintō."[2] Modern scholarship has shown quite conclusively that Shintō

---

2. The title "*Saiin*" and its equivalent, "*Itsuki no miya*," have sometimes been rendered as "Kamo Virgin" (as *Saigū*, the title of the High Priestess of Ise, is often rendered "Ise Virgin"). Like the Vestal Virgins, these priestesses were of royal birth, often appointed in early childhood or, at any rate, before puberty, and the maintenance of virginal purity was one of the expectations of a serving Saiin or Saigū. Some Kamo and Ise priestesses in both history and fiction are said to have had their amorous adventures, even while in service, but none of the stories about Senshi suggest that her virginity was ever lost.

and Buddhism were hardly ever distinct, at least not until a process of forcibly separating the two traditions and their institutions was begun in the Tokugawa period and completed by a series of government actions in the Meiji, Taishō, and Shōwa eras.[3] Neil McMullin, summarizing his view of the Buddhist/Shintō relationship in premodern times (from the middle of the Heian period to Meiji), has gone so far as to state that "all so-called Buddhist institutions were at least partly Shintō, and all so-called Shintō institutions were at least partly Buddhist. In other words, all major religious institutions in Japan combined both Buddhist and Shintō elements in complex, integrated wholes. This institutional amalgam both reflected and generated the Buddhist-Shintō doctrinal and ritual synthesis."[4] To obtain such a view, scholars have attempted to circumvent Tokugawa-period and later views of the relationship and to replace them with an image constructed from evidence produced in earlier times and found in a wide variety of materials, including literary texts. *Hosshin wakashū*, a devout Buddhist literary work by a laywoman who was in the middle of her extremely long term of service as High Priestess of Kamo when she wrote it, would seem to offer itself as a likely piece of evidence in support of this image of the confluence of the two religious streams. But in fact things are not quite that simple.

If anything, *Hosshin wakashū* reveals a consciousness of differentiation, of limits on the integration of the two traditions at one particular juncture. At least insofar as their relationship is depicted in this cycle of poems by this particular High Priestess, Kamo—one particular manifestation of Shintō as it was constituted in the late tenth and early eleventh centuries—and Buddhism were by no means at ease with each other. It might be said that such tensions as seem to have existed between them are precisely what *Hosshin wakashū* is all about. We must remember that what we read in such a text is not necessarily history per se, but rather literature produced by a historical personage in historical times, subject to the

---

3. In Western scholarship, the pivotal contribution to the new understanding of the Buddhist/Shintō relationship was Kuroda Toshio's "Shintō in the History of Japanese Religion" in *The Journal of Japanese Studies* 7.1 (Winter 1981): 1–21. Other important articles relating to this problem are: Allan G. Grapard, "Japan's Ignored Cultural Revolution: The Separation of Shintō and Buddhist Divinities in Meiji (*shinbutsu bunri*) and a Case Study: Tōnomine" in *History of Religions* 23.3 (February 1984): 240–65, and "Institution, Ritual and Ideology: The Twenty-Two Shrine-Temple Multiplexes of Heian Japan" in *History of Religions* 27.3 (February 1988): 246–69; and Neil McMullin, "Historical and Historiographical Issues in the Study of Pre-Modern Japanese Religion" in *Japanese Journal of Religious Studies* 16.1 (March 1989): 3–40 (see especially 4–8).

4. McMullin, ibid., 8.

influences of literary convention as well as those of artistic invention. But a particular kind of formal constraint upon the Buddhist/Shintō relationship is certainly one of the major topics of Senshi's literary works, and it could not have functioned so viably as a literary topic had it not shared or overlapped with some of the contours of her life experience (whatever they were).

It is no doubt true that men and women of Senshi's time experienced and understood the relationship between the two religious traditions in very different ways from those of Tokugawa figures like Motoori Norinaga (1730–1801), but it may also be true that the relationship of certain Shintō institutions to Buddhist ones may have varied from one period to another, and that in certain periods some Shintō institutions—Kamo, for instance—may not have had the same relationship to Buddhism as did other institutions at that same time. To be sure, Kamo was one of a group of twenty-two major shrines (*nijūnisha*) that from early Heian times were paired with important adjacent Buddhist temples that also received imperial patronage (the temple associated with the Kamo Shrines was called the Kamo Jingūji; it no longer exists).[5] Also, like many another Shintō deity, one of the *kami* worshiped at Kamo, "Kamo Daimyōjin," was often identified as a manifestation of a major Buddhist deity, in this case the bodhisattva Kannon (Avalokiteśvara).[6] But there were also some special

---

5. Grapard, "Institution, Ritual, and Ideology," 249, 253; *Kokushi daijiten* Henshū Iinkai, ed., *Kokushi daijiten* 3 (Tokyo: Yoshikawa Kōbunkan, 1983), 614.

6. The fifth volume of *Kojidan*, an early Kamakura-period tale collection (compiled by Minamoto Akikane between 1212 and 1215), contains what appears to be the first instance of this particular identification—and ample illustration of the kind of amalgam of practices and beliefs described by McMullin. According to this tale, the scholar and poet Fujiwara Norikane (1107–65) was assigned administrative duties at the Kamo Shrine, and each time that he presented himself at the shrine he made an offering of a copy of the "Heart Sutra" (*Shingyō*. From the earliest stages of the development of Japanese Buddhism, this sutra was one of those most frequently copied for offertory purposes by devout laypersons. See also the discussion of *HSWKS* poem 5, below.) Norikane prospered as a result, and after a point was able to have all the offertory copies of the sutra executed in gold ink. Then, during an all-night vigil at the shrine, a beautiful female figure appeared to him. Of this apparition Norikane requested, first, that he might receive a promotion to higher rank, and also that he might not die before his mother. Then he asked, "What is the Buddhist manifestation (*honji*) of the Kamo deity?" whereupon the female figure turned into an image of Kannon (i.e., *Shō Kannon*, the "main" form of the bodhisattva rather than one of the many esoteric forms) holding a lotus flower. In the next instant, the image burst into flame and disintegrated into cinder and ash. Soon thereafter, Norikane had a similar image of Kannon made, and he presented it to the Tōzandō, one of the worship halls in the Kamo precincts. Subsequently, he did receive his promotion and also outlived his mother, and his descendants also prospered: all of this was attributed to the workings of Kamo Daimyōjin. *Kojidan*, in Kuroita Katsumi, ed., *Shintei zōho kokushi taikei* 18 (Tokyo: *Kokushi taikei* Kankōkai, 1932), 100.

ways in which the two religious streams were kept apart at Kamo as they were at Ise (which also had its own counterpart Buddhist institution and a Buddha to match its chief deity). The women who served as High Priestesses in these two cults—almost always imperial princesses—and the women and men who served them were expected to restrict their behavior and even their speech in various ways and thus were to keep Buddhism and its symbols, language, and adherents from tainting their own persons and precincts. Kuroda Toshio has suggested that the prohibition against speaking about Buddhism that prevailed at Ise "in fact does not imply a rejection of Buddhism but rather indicates a special attitude or etiquette assumed in the presence of the *kami*."[7] This may be so—and may be a good reason for replacing the word "taboo" in discussions of these customs with something more like "habits or strategies of abstinence"—but it does not change the fact that these rules or customs were widely recognized and must certainly have altered the consciousness, if not the actual manners and speech, of women and men serving in these institutions. If not actually curtailed, their contacts with Buddhist monks and nuns (including family members and former colleagues), their participation in the kinds of rites that other lay women and men took part in, and even their private acts of devotion (prayer, meditation, sutra reading or copying, if they did that much) must have taken on a special character, and must have been carried out with some sense of otherness vis-à-vis other women and men of comparable status or class.

It remains difficult to say how strictly these restrictions or regulations (some, as shall be seen, were set forth in legal codes) were actually observed, and again one may assume that in certain times and in certain situations they may have been more strictly observed than at others. But it is certain that from Heian through Tokugawa times, people writing about the Kamo institution, from both inside and outside, were cognizant of these special, delimiting guidelines and saw fit to document various ways in which they were made manifest in behavior and practice. One of the earliest extant Kamo chronicles, the *Kamo Kōtaijingū ki* ("Records of the Imperial Kamo Shrines"), the oldest copy of which dates to 1405, concludes with some discussion of the verbal and other abstinences.[8] As

---

7. Kuroda Toshio, "Shintō in the History of Japanese Religion," 13.

8. For a text, see Hanawa Hokiichi, ed., *Gunsho ruijū* 1 (Tokyo: Keizai Zasshisha, 1898), (Jingibu 15), 518–27. The author of the *Kamo Kōtaijingū ki* is not known, but it appears to be the sort of anecdotal chronicle that would have been written by hereditary shrine officials as documentation of the various traditions of the institution, thereby instilling those traditions with an aura of antiquarian authority. A similar, later document is the *Kamo chūshin zakki* of 1680, discussed below.

evidence of their gravity it cites a poem by Senshi (to be discussed in detail below) that has always been understood as a silent protest against them, and continues with an anecdote about a still better known poet, the famous monk Saigyō (1118–90): before he became a monk, it seems, Saigyō had been a faithful Kamo devotee; but late in life, while he was in the western provinces on one of his many pilgrimages, he realized that it had been a long time since he had paid his respects at Kamo and worried whether he would live long enough to do so, and so he returned to the capital forthwith. He made his visit to Kamo on the night of the tenth day of the tenth month of the second year of the Nin'an era (1167[9]), but since he was now a monk and his physical presence in the precincts therefore prohibited (*imitamau yue ni*), he did not enter but stopped outside at the Tanao Shrine (a subsidiary of the Upper Kamo Shrine) and asked that his offering be made by intermediaries. The moonlight filtering down through the dense trees around the shrine made the mood of the moment and the place seem even more supernaturally charged (*kamisabiwatarite*) than usual. Deeply moved, Saigyō composed the following poem:

> *kashikomaru shide ni namida no kakaru ka na*
> *mata itsu ka mo to omou aware ni*
> Tears fall on the strands of paper that are my offering,
> from my grief at the thought that I may never come again.

The authors of the *Kamo Kōtaijingū ki* seem to have played a little fast and loose with this poem: although the *kotobagaki* attached to it in various earlier *waka* collections in which it appears (including *Sankashū*, the major collection of Saigyō's own works, and *Gyokuyō wakashū*, a *chokusenshū* compiled in 1312[10]) are essentially similar, all have "*mata itsu ka wa to omou*" instead of "*mata itsu ka mo*" in the poem. The meaning is the same (literally, "thinking 'when shall I come again?'"), but the version in the Kamo chronicle makes it appear that Saigyō has cleverly and intentionally embedded the name of the Kamo Shrine itself in the poem he offered in lieu of personal performance of the act of worship. "It was thus," explains the chronicle, "because the name of the Buddha and the like were prohibited (*imitamau*) in both the Ise and the Kamo Shrines. However, if one's prayers are made with a sincere heart, is there any reason why they should not be

---

9. Some versions of the same story give Nin'an 3 (1168) as the date.

10. See *Gyokuyō wakashū* 2786 and *Sankashū* 1094 in *Shinpen kokka taikan* (*Shinpen kokka taikan* Henshū Iinkai, ed., *Shinpen kokka taikan* 1 [Tokyo: Kadokawa Shoten, 1983], 480, and vol. 3, 594. Volumes in this series will hereafter be cited as *SKT*).

fulfilled?"[11] The implication is that Saigyō's offering was as good as anybody's, even if the fact that he was a Buddhist monk forced him to alter the manner of presentation. Thus, this Kamo chronicle, like others of its kind, acknowledges the special facets of Kamo/Buddhist relations and documents their durability, yet at the same time seems to play down their ultimate effect. It may be that this very ambivalence is, after all, the most telling thing about this tale.

The enduring image of Senshi that emerges in portrayals, both in traditional literature and in modern writing about her, is likewise of a woman who managed herself remarkably well in a terribly ambivalent situation: she found ways to serve both the Kamo gods and the state, on the one hand, and to pursue, express, and share her Buddhist faith with almost all who came in contact with her. But she was certainly no Sor Juana Inés de la Cruz: no authorities ever forced her to give up one side of her life for another, or silenced her poetic voice out of fear of the influence her poems might have on others.[12] Was ambivalence really a great burden that Senshi had to bear through most of her life, or was it essentially a peculiar poetic position in which to stand and voice certain sentiments, whether real or fabricated, or exaggerated? Did she really believe as she wrote, even about such things as the special handicaps that face women in Buddhism (of this, more below), or were such thematic and topical manipulations simply more deft handling of the array of poetic figures that lay at her disposal and presented themselves as apt for her use?

Perhaps both ways of understanding her are helpful. And it may be that her devotion to and absorption in *waka*—as art and pastime, as a mode of communication, as a valuable skill imparted graciously and authoritatively to younger women—were just as great as her devotion to her official duties or to her Buddhist goals, and maybe even greater. Writing *Hosshin wakashū* may not have perfectly reconciled these competing interests—if indeed they were in competition—but perhaps it was a way of creating a kind of textual arena in which they all might meet and in which their points of contact could be exposed. Such tensions as may have existed among them, if only in some formal or figurative sense, might then be made much of, for poetic and dramatic effect, and might also through such manipulation be diminished.

---

11. Hanawa Hokiichi, ed., *Gunsho ruijū* 5, 526–27.

12. Octavio Paz's *Sor Juana, or The Traps of Faith* (Cambridge: The Belknap Press of Harvard University Press, 1988) is one recent study of this great Mexican poet (1651?–95), a Hieronymite nun who in 1693 was forced by church fathers to give up the studies of philosophy, science, and secular literature that had been the sources of inspiration for her own works. She apparently accepted the demand that she be silent: though prolific up to that time, she wrote nothing whatsoever in the last two years of her life.

But, as we shall see, the thematic progression played out in her cycle of Buddhist poems ends not in reconciled peace and the assured anticipation of bliss but in a suspension, a state of lingering doubt still undercutting the desire to believe and hope wholeheartedly. The text might come to an end, but the work would have to go on: faith would continue to require nurture of the kind offered in *Hosshin wakashū*, and more. The final reward for the effort would not come in this life, but in the life to come; yet in the meantime, there might be other satisfactions, such as those enjoyed through the sharing of these poems and others like them. Though this is the only such cycle that Senshi is known to have written, it might well have served as the model for many more, by Senshi and others.

It may also have served in one other way as well: it is possible that in some way Senshi's composition of these poems may have led to a transformation in one aspect of the *waka* tradition itself. Up until her own time, *Shakkyōka* had not yet become part of the canon as defined by the range of topics and modes included in the official anthologies. But perhaps because poets like Senshi sought and found ways to adapt the canonical, secular *waka* to Buddhist contexts, in admirable acts of composition presented as sincere devotional exercises, this eventually changed: a place was made in the anthologies, beginning with the fourth, the *Goshūi wakashū*—compiled in 1086, about five decades after her death—for a few such poems, and eventually some of the *chokusenshū Shakkyōka* sections included some of her own poems as well.[13] Thus, what had once been treated as peripheral was brought to the center. The inclusion of "Buddhist poems" like Senshi's in the anthologies compiled in the centuries after her death marks the acceptance of such poetry as a distinguished compositional mode, a shift made possible, in part, by the transfer of such prestige as her own to a type of *waka* with which she, perhaps somewhat ironically, had come to be so very closely identified.

---

13. For a study and translation of the *Shakkyōka* subsection in the *Goshūi wakashū*, see Robert E. Morrell, "The Buddhist Poetry in the *Goshūishū*" in *Monumenta Nipponica* 28.1 (Spring 1973): 87–100. The *HSWKS* poems included in *chokusenshū* are listed below in part two, n. 1.

PART ONE
THE GREAT KAMO PRIESTESS

"**A**mong the many women who served over the ages as Kamo priestess (*Saiin*) there were none who did not compose poetry." So observed the latter-day male officials of the Kamo Shrines who wrote *Kamo chūshin zakki*, an anecdotal history of their institution, in 1680 (Enpō 8).[1] Though they were writing about an office that was occupied for just over four hundred years by some thirty-five different women of royal blood, they named only two Kamo priestesses as representatives of this collective literary achievement. Their first example, Uchiko Naishinnō (807–47), the very first Saiin, was indeed "skilled in the ways of poetry of both Japan and China (*Yamato Morokoshi no fumi no michi ni mo tsūjitamaeri*)," and the *Kamo chūshin zakki* authors duly quoted the poem in Chinese (*shi*) that Uchiko wrote in the spring of 823 when her father, the emperor Saga, paid a state visit to the Kamo Shrines.[2] The seventeen-year-old Uchiko's vivid description of the solitude of her life as Kamo priestess ("Silent was my lonely lodge among the mountain trees") is typical of literary accounts of the Saiin as a place removed both spatially and psychologically from court, the source and locus of light and goodness embodied here, as so often, in the person of the emperor who has graced her residence with his presence.[3] The final lines of the poem ("If I should once more know the warmth of this fair face/ all my life I will give thanks to the azure skies")

---

1. *Kamo chūshin zakki* (hereafter "*Zakki*") was compiled under the direction of the high priest (*kannushi*) Okamoto Yasuyoshi. For the passage cited here, see Kokusho Kankōkai, ed., *Zoku zoku gunsho ruijū* 1: *Jingibu* (Tokyo: Kokusho Kankōkai, 1906), 603b.

2. The visit is recorded in *Nihon kiryaku*, Kōnin 14.2.28. See Kuroita Katsumi, ed., *Shintei zōho kokushi taikei* 10 (Tokyo: *Kokushi taikei* Kankōkai, 1929), 313–14. For the text of the poem, see Ichikawa Kansai, ed., *Nihon shiki* (Tokyo: Kokusho Kankōkai, 1911), 23.

3. Burton Watson, trans., *Japanese Literature in Chinese, vol. 1: Poetry and Prose by Japanese Writers of the Early Period* (New York and London: Columbia University Press, 1975), 46.
   The word *Saiin* was used for the institutional office of High Priestess of the Kamo Shrine, for her residence (separate from the shrine itself), and for the woman who occupied that office and that residence. The term will be used herein in a similar manner. In several poems by Senshi and her Saiin companions (for example, *Daisaiin saki no gyoshū* nos. 12 and 25; see *SKT* 3, 279), the priestess's residence is referred to as a *yamazato*, an isolated mountain dwelling-place. Though conventional, this trope relates the sense of separation and reclusion inherent in Saiin life, and this idea is as suitable in these *waka* as it is in Uchiko's *shi*.

are not just a daughter's declaration of affection and respect for her father but also an admission of the Saiin's sense of physical and social isolation.

"The emperor praised this poem, and for generations it has been recited with admiration," the *Zakki* authors report, and then make what at first seems an abrupt shift in topic:

> The subject of the taboos (*gyokinki*) customarily observed by the Kamo priestesses in recognition of the importance of their divine service appears in certain of their writings. Since this country is, originally, a country of *kami*, the priestesses avoided the very words "Buddha," "Buddhist teachings," and "Buddhist clergy" [*Buppōsō*], and were so careful about their language that they called the Buddha "*Nakago*," the sutras "*somekami*," pagodas "*araragi*," Buddhist priests "*kaminaga*" and nuns "*mekaminaga*," and referred to the Buddhist monk's single daily meal—which the monk calls "*toki*"—as "*katasonae*."[4]

The purpose of this discussion of verbal taboos and approved euphemisms only becomes clear after what appears to be yet another abrupt shift. The *Zakki* authors are now ready to introduce their other example of a distinguished Saiin poet, although they have begun to explain her poem even before mentioning her name.

> The daughter of the emperor Murakami who served as Saiin was named Senshi Naishinnō. All of the women who served as Saiin were women who were not as yet married. Also, if anything were to mar their purity, they were made to withdraw from service. But this Saiin—perhaps because she understood the will of the *kami* so well— served for as long as fifty-four years [*sic*].[5] She keenly sensed the mutability and the transience of this world, but, it is said, she composed the following poem to show that, though she had conceived of a desire for Buddhist enlightenment (*Bodaishin o hosshitamaedomo*), she still could not bring the Buddha into her life of service to the gods:

> *omoedomo imu to te iwanu koto nareba*
> *sonata ni mukite ne o nomi zo naku*
> Though I think about it, it is taboo, a thing not to be said,
>   and so all that I can do is turn in that direction and weep.[6]

---

4. *Zakki*, 603b. Unless otherwise noted, all translations are the author's.

5. Senshi actually served for fifty-seven years. See below pp. 29, 51–52.

6. *Zakki*, 604a.

Like Uchiko's *shi*, this is Senshi's most frequently quoted poem, and it lent itself naturally to the *Zakki* authors' attempt to document a tradition of Saiin poetry with just two examples.[7] Also, like Uchiko's *shi*, Senshi's *tanka* also speaks of isolation—in this case, the Saiin's unique isolation from Buddhism, a special problem for the Kamo priestesses of which this poem is perhaps the best emblem. The problem is represented within the poem by the reference to a special rule of abstinence (*imi*) that ostensibly governed habits of speech in the Saiin environment, and the way that the poem is introduced in the *Zakki* is typical of commentaries on it, in that it focuses on this element, the thing that makes the poem unusual and somehow especially representative of the putative Saiin poetic tradition. But for some reason the *Zakki* authors presented the poem without the *kotobagaki* (prose introduction) with which it is almost always encountered and upon which almost all commentaries on the poem depend. The earliest appearance of both the *kotobagaki* and the poem is in the last book ("miscellaneous poems") of *Shika wakashū*, the sixth *chokusenshū*, or imperial anthology of Japanese poetry, compiled by Fujiwara Akisuke between 1151 and 1174, over one hundred years after Senshi's death, where it is presented like this:

> *Kamo no itsuki to kikoekeru toki ni nishi ni mukaite yomeru*
>   *Senshi Naishinnō*
> *omoedomo imu to te iwanu koto nareba*
>   *sonata ni mukite ne o nomi zo naku*[8]

Translated, the *kotobagaki* says, "A poem composed while she was Kamo priestess, as she faced west." Twelfth-century readers of *Shika wakashū*, aided by this *kotobagaki* and recognizing the name of the poet that appeared along with it, must have understood this poem readily. Today, a little more explanation is needed in order to understand what is going on here—to understand what the *kotobagaki* and the poem together "tell" us, to perceive what it is that makes the poem a poem, other than its thirty-one-syllable *tanka* form, and to see why discussions of Senshi's Buddhist poetry inevitably begin with this one poem.

---

7. There does seem to have been an enduring association between the Kamo cult and the *waka* tradition. The *Kamo Kōtaijingū ki* names Fujiwara Shunzei (1112–1204) as the example of many individuals who received guidance in the "way of Japanese poetry" (*shikishima no michi*) from the Kamo deity, and reports that, in search of fulfillment of his prayer that his descendants might inherit his success in *waka* as art and profession for many generations, he visited and prayed at the Kamo Shrine each day for one thousand days in succession (*Kamo Kōtaijingū ki*, in Hanawa, ed., *Gunsho ruijū* 15, 523).

8. See *SKT* 1, 183.

As a unit, the *kotobagaki* and the poem "tell" us this: at the time of the composition of the poem, the poet, Senshi, a woman of royal birth, was High Priestess of the Kamo Shrines (*Kamo no itsuki,* i.e., *Saiin*), an imperial emissary to the native deities, guardian and symbol of the purity of the shrines themselves. And at the moment of the composition of the poem, this woman turned to the west (*nishi ni mukaite*), an action immediately recognizable as a gesture of reverence toward Amida Buddha's Pure Land, the most sought-after afterlife goal of Japanese Buddhists, attainable, according to Amida Buddha's vows, through sincere expressions of faith in him. The poet then uttered, or silently "thought," or otherwise composed (*yomu*) this poem.

The first word of the poem, *omoedomo,* means, "I think about it, but . . ." or "I yearn for it/ to do it, but . . ." Senshi, *thinking about* or *yearning for* the Pure Land, or thinking or yearning for Amida, *intends to* utter his name, but "to do so [most literally, 'to utter that name'] is a thing to be abstained from" (*imu to te*), and so that name, "Amida Buddha," is "a thing/word (*koto*) that cannot be spoken." (As the *Zakki* authors explained, custom, though not law itself, forbade the utterance of the word "Buddha" [*butsu, hotoke*], and other defiling words like "to die" [*shinu*] and "blood" [*chi*] in the Saiin precincts.) "And so," says the poem, "since that name is something that cannot be said [*iwanu koto nareba*], I can do nothing but turn my face in that direction [*sonata ni mukite*]"—the direction, west (*nishi*), specified by context, not by word—"and weep [*ne o nomi zo naku*]."

By itself, for any reader, the meaning of this poem may have been, and may be, hard to grasp. But when read with the *kotobagaki* or some other gloss, the meaning of its problematic elements—*imu to te, sonata ni mukite, ne o nomi zo naku* (*What* word is taboo? Facing *which* direction? *Why* the tears?)—and of the poem as a whole becomes almost too obvious. Is this a poem that could only be understood when glossed as it was by the *kotobagaki* attached to it in the *Shika wakashū*, or by the explanatory introduction given it by the *Zakki* authors? Can it now only be understood when glossed as above, or in one or another way that gives it context? Perhaps. What, then, makes it a poem, if its meaning can only be retrieved or reconstructed through these extrinsic appurtenances? (Nothing like such a question may have occurred to the *Shika wakashū* editor or the *Zakki* authors, but it is an important question for us.) For one thing, there is its diction, which, besides conveying literal meanings (meanings that may only be retrievable through reliance on the extrinsic appurtenances, as is most obvious in the case of the nonspecific *sonata,* made specific by the context provided by the *kotobagaki,* which literally supplies the equivalent *nishi*), is what makes this a poem like other poems, or at least, a Japanese poem like other Japanese poems. That first word, *omoedomo,* might be the first word of a love poem—"I yearn for him/ I think about him . . . [but there is some problem or obstacle, he does not come, I cannot see him]"—but it is not a love poem in the usual sense. The object yearned for is Amida Buddha, or his Pure Land, or access to them. The last words of the poem are tautologically poetic, for "*ne o naku*" is a formulaic substitute for or embellishment of the verb "*naku*," "weep." The use of such language is one of the poet's ways of showing that this is a poem, and that it has something in common with countless other *waka* in which "*ne o naku*" conveys the sorrow of frustrated lovers, homesick travelers, and other mourners.[9]

What is also poetic—what must have seemed so to the anthologizer, and what should seem so to us, if we accept what we are told about the context—is the "fact," documented by both the *kotobagaki* and the poem itself, that the poet has expressed herself, about her situation and feelings, in a poem, using the form of the *tanka*, and that she has done so in the kind of language evolved and approved for use in *waka* by centuries of tradition. The poet's subject—what she has to say—is not conventionally the stuff of Japanese verse, but the way she says it is very much so, in fact very typical of a broad range of poems that express feelings of dissatisfaction, frustration, or inability to achieve objects of desire.[10] Whether so labeled or not, a *jukkai* ("expressing one's feelings") poem creates its own context: the poet documents his or her emotional condition, which is the poem's context, however explicit or inexplicit it may be.

There can be little question that these are her own feelings Senshi is expressing in this poem, though there is, of course, no word in the poem that corresponds to the word "I" used in the translation. But beginning as it does with the verb *omou*, which tells us that someone is thinking or feeling something, and ending with the emotive, emphatic *ne o nomi zo naku*, the poem is most naturally read as a first-person utterance—or rather, the readable representation of what ideally could be one. This

---

9. See, for example, *Man'yōshū* no. 481, where "*ne nomi zo nak[u]*" is preceded by a *makurakotoba*, "*asadori no*," suggesting that the poet's cries for his dead wife resemble those of morning birds, as well as *Man'yōshū* nos. 897–98, *Ise monogatari* section 65 (". . . *warekara to ne o koso nakame yo o ba uramiji*"—"I grieve that it was my own fault, and shall not blame the world") or *Kokin wakashū* no. 536:

Ausaka no yūtsukedori mo waga gotoshi
   hito ya koishi ne nomi nakuran
Is the cock at the Ausaka Barrier crying like that as I do,
   out of longing for someone?

These poems are quoted from the editions in the *Nihon koten bungaku taikei* (hereafter *NKBT*), 100 vols. (Tokyo: Iwanami Shoten, 1957–69).

10. Poems of this conventional type most frequently are complaints about aging or loss of status. For a discussion of the place of *jukkai* poems in Heian *waka* composition, see Minegishi Yoshiaki, *Heian jidai waka bungaku no kenkyū* (Tokyo: Ōfūsha, 1966), 290–328.

reading is further supported (or suggested) by the *kotobagaki* and the indication of the poet's name, as one reads them together in the anthology: they prompt one to read the poem as not simply some individual person's utterance but as the utterance of a particular person, Senshi, a "she" about whom we can think, speak, and write. She was a woman of high repute in the late tenth and early eleventh centuries, a public figure and a literary tastemaker, so to twelfth-century readers the very appearance of her name beside this poem may have been enough to educe certain associations that would strongly color their reading of the poem. Later readers, too, might draw on knowledge of her gained through their reading of other works, especially accounts of her in *rekishi-monogatari* (semihistorical narratives) and in collections of *setsuwa* (anecdotal tales), and might bring this knowledge to their reading of the poem, too. In almost every encounter with the poem, the *kotobagaki* and the author's name would also be there, extrapoetic appurtenances preparing the reading of the poem, making sure that the process of reading it would always be preceded by a fixing in the mind of the reader of the notion that this poem was written by a real, particular, knowable person and that knowledge of this, and of the circumstances in which she wrote it ("*Kamo no itsuki to kikoekeru toki ni . . .*") was a key to any reading and understanding of the poem itself.

In the *Zakki* presentation of the poem the poet as historical persona was especially important—perhaps more so than the poem. But quoting the poem's *kotobagaki* apparently did not serve the *Zakki* authors' purpose—any more than it did those of the anonymous authors of the much earlier *Kamo Kōtaijingū ki.*[11] It may be too much to suppose that they perceived that inclusion of the *kotobagaki* might make the whole quotation incriminating or embarrassing, but there certainly have been those who have read the *kotobagaki* and the poem in that sort of light. In the late eighteenth century, when Motoori Norinaga (1730–1801) read the words "*Kamo no itsuki to kikoekeru toki ni . . .*" and then read the poem as he found them in *Shika wakashū*, he expressed great indignation—almost disgust— at the very idea that Senshi, in these circumstances, should have expressed such sentiments as these in this way. His short essay on Senshi's poem, included in his miscellany *Tamakatsuma*,[12] is an extended gloss on *imu to te*, the words in the poem that most need explication, but, as one

---

11. See the discussion in the prologue, above.

12. Norinaga began writing and compiling *Tamakatsuma* in 1793, and it was published in parts at various times through 1812. For an annotated edition, see Yoshikawa Kōjirō, Satake Akihiro, and Hino Tatsuo, eds., *Motoori Norinaga* (Nihon shisō taikei 40) (Tokyo: Iwanami Shoten, 1978).

might expect, it is also a complaint against the pollution of Shintō institutions by Buddhism:

> In the habitations of the Ise and Kamo priestesses, Buddhism was strictly taboo, and even the utterance of words having anything to do with it was officially forbidden. However, the people of this nation—the high and the low, the wise and the ignorant—all, without exception, believed in the teachings of the Buddha, and it became the custom to make bitter lamentation over the fact that service to the gods was a terribly sinful thing. Now, in order to serve the gods with true devotion, such resentment should not have been entertained under any circumstances, but this turning to the west in tears was an unspeakable abomination [*iwamu kata naki magakoto ni zo arikeru*]. In outward appearance she was devoted to the divine ancestral gods, but the heart within her was devoted exclusively to Amida. Even if she nurtured such sentiments in her heart, since there was this strict official prohibition, she should not have revealed her feelings in poetry. And even if she did compose such poems, she certainly should not have told anyone about them. How ashamed she must have been![13]

It would have been one thing, in Norinaga's view, if Senshi had kept her yearning within her heart (*onkokoro no uchi*), but she went too far when she voiced that yearning in this poem. Norinaga equated the act of composition with an act of communication, "telling others about it" (*hito ni katari*), "revealing it in [the composition of] a poem" (*uta nado ni yomiarawashita-mau*). An inside-outside dialectic is also at work in his description of Senshi, with her "outward appearance" (*onkatachi*) as a servant of the gods concealing the devotion to Amida that she nurtured in her heart (*onkokoro*). But, in his view, the time-honored justification of poetry as a means for releasing to the outside world that which would otherwise be pent up inside is not to be extended to Senshi if it is this kind of thing that she had to express. The conventions of poetic confession, in Norinaga's view, have allowed Senshi to admit to feelings that she should have kept to herself.

Still, Norinaga is willing to excuse this hypocritical trespass against official strictures (*omoki imashime*) as an act of conformity with societal norms, misbegotten though they may have been, and he wonders if the gods themselves would not have been equally forgiving:

---

13. Ibid., 91–92.

But this princess was not the only one to err in this way. Even the wisest of people thought it was a splendid thing to ignore the gods and revere and practice the teachings of the Buddha exclusively, for it was the custom in that society to say and think that this Buddhism was a means by which one might learn sensitivity [*kokoro fukaku aware naru waza*]. Now, this princess was known as *"Daisaiin"* because she served as priestess through five reigns, from that of Emperor En'yū, in the Ten'en era, to that of Goichijō, in the Chōgen era, until she was close to the age of seventy. Given the customs of that time, it was perfectly reasonable for her to be terribly distressed by the fact that she was unable to practice the way of the Buddha until she had reached that advanced age. But surely the gods, acknowledging her long, untiring service to them, would have taken pity on this princess who gave so much of her heart to the Buddha [*nakago ni onkokoro yosete*] and "turned to the west to weep," for they would have seen that this was the custom of her time. Or perhaps all this, too, was the doing of those mischief-makers among the gods [*magatsubi no kami*].[14]

So this *magagoto*, a perverse act, may really have been the work of *magatsubi no kami*, wayward spirits leading Senshi astray. Thus, Norinaga generously suggests that this otherwise admirable woman may not herself have been responsible for this one reprehensible act that happens to be recorded in a *kotobagaki* and poem in *Shika wakashū*. In fact, his main object in this essay in *Tamakatsuma* would appear to have been to use the poem as an example of the kind of syncretic religious practices and attitudes of which he took such a dim view (underscored by his use of the conventional euphemism when referring to Senshi's devotion to the Buddha) rather than to comment on the poem itself or on the poet.

We may be tempted to take Norinaga to task for the biases and anachronisms in this analysis, and other critics have done so.[15] But what we must notice first is that his reading of the poem takes its cue entirely from the *kotobagaki*: the information that it gives him is ineluctable, and what he does say about the poem is as much a commentary on the *kotobagaki* as it is a commentary on the poem itself. There may have been no other way that he could have read the poem, since it came to him equipped with this information—information that put him on the offensive so far as the poem was concerned, even before he read the poem itself. And there may have

---

14. Ibid.

15. See, for example, Yamazato Keiseki, "Daisaiin Senshi Naishinnō no Bukkyō," *Ryūkoku shidan* 56–57 (December 1966): 373–400; and Okazaki Tomoko, "Daisaiin Senshi no kenkyū" in her *Heian joryū sakka no kenkyū* (Kyoto: Hōzōkan, 1967), 140–41.

been other factors that set his mind against the poem: it is not unlikely, for instance, that Norinaga's encounter with the poem would have been influenced by what Kitamura Kigin (1624–1705) had to say about it in his annotated edition of *Shika wakashū* (in *Hachidaishū shō*).[16] Kigin's headnote was also essentially an informative gloss on *imu to te*, but it was far less judgmental: "In Shintō, Buddhism is taboo; the scriptures and the Buddhas, for example, are called *somekami* and *nakago*. Since, therefore, she could not perform the *nenbutsu*, she just turned toward the west and sat facing it, weeping."[17] This comment, too, is launched by the indication in the *kotobagaki* that the poem was written "while she was Kamo Priestess": that historical and situational context serves as the key to the meaning of *imu to te*, the part of the poem that both Kigin and Norinaga felt most compelled to explain. (Actually, Kigin's examples of euphemisms employed in place of certain Buddhist words are rather tangential.) But without the *kotobagaki* and such other knowledge as they may have had about the author of the poem, one wonders, would Kigin have explained *imu to te* in quite this way, and would Norinaga have been likely to have taken any notice of this poem at all? The power of a *kotobagaki* to steer interpretation in one direction or another is not to be underestimated, nor is the way that it can interact with such predispositions as the reader may bring to the reading of a poem.

Anthologies of Japanese poetry would no doubt be harder to read, and perhaps far less interesting, without *kotobagaki*, and the role that they play in the reading of poems is one that bears close examination. The *kotobagaki* attached to poems in the selective anthologies (*chokusenshū* and other *senshū*), beginning with the *Man'yōshū*, ostensibly inform the reader about some aspect of the moments in which the poems they introduce were conceived and created. Many *kotobagaki* are relatively explicit about time, place, and person (even when they simply identify the particular *utaawase*, or poetry contest, or other occasion on which the poem was composed, or simply name the topic), whereas these matters generally have no place in the poems themselves; the rarefied diction of *waka* for the most part precludes them. But the compilers of the selective anthologies—in some cases, though not always, the authors of the *kotobagaki*—expected their readers to read the *kotobagaki* and the poems together as units consisting of two parts in which two different kinds of language record and convey both "historical" information and "lyrical"

---

16. *Hachidaishū shō*, Kigin's edition with commentary on the "imperial anthologies of eight reigns," was published in 1682. See Yamagishi Tokuhei, ed., *Hachidaishū zenchū*, 3 vols. (Tokyo: Yūseidō, 1960).

17. Ibid., vol. 2, 295.

expression about events or experiences that are thus presented as "real," even if they are but partially so. Even when a poem was recited from memory, in isolation from its *kotobagaki*, the unuttered *kotobagaki* attached to it in the anthology from which it was learned must have done much to shape the reciter's comprehension of the meaning of the poem and his or her nostalgic (and often imaginary) impression of the original poet's sentiments and circumstances at the moment of composition.

Once anthologized and equipped with *kotobagaki*, poems became virtually inseparable from the temporal and situational contexts thereby provided for them. The poem could no longer be read (if it ever could be) simply as language at play (or, perhaps we should say, at work) in the expression of feeling, sensation, or comprehension. It was now a record of the "fact" of its own composition, an historical artifact (which is one of the things it may have been in the first place). The equipping of the poem with such an apparatus was part of the historical process whereby poems became coated with layered effects of the many acts of reading, interpretation, classification, and annotation performed on them. Recollection and recitation of, or allusion to, any given poem thus invariably involves the recollection and reiteration of the many-layered appurtenance which that poem bears. The evocation of nostalgic sentiment through such recollection was always and still is one of the primary objectives of that recollection; another might be the creation of a new poem, the language and sentiments of which would be linked to those of the recollected poem. The value of such recollection, then, was positive, though often bittersweet; the Japanese word *aware*, with all its ambiguity, may be the word that best describes the emotional force of such acts of recollection and recreation.

A great part of the nostalgia involved in these acts would focus on the person of the poet, no matter how obscure or fictitious. The creation or recreation of a sense that he or she was at one time in such circumstances—physical, social, psychological—as described in greater or lesser detail in the *kotobagaki*, and that he or she thereby or therefore was moved to write the poem that follows, is the very object of the writing of the *kotobagaki* itself. When the poet's name is included, a creator's persona emerges in sharper focus, but even when the poet is unknown and unnameable—*yomibito shirazu*, as the anthologizers are so often compelled to record where they would otherwise wish to record a name for that persona—he or she is still a presence, however empty or anonymous, in the presentation of the poem. To say that the name of the poet is not known by no means lessens the power of the suggestion that there was a poet who wrote the poem and who could at least potentially be named if known, and the willingness to record the words *yomibito shirazu* in place of the poet's name indicates how important such naming was to the anthologizers.

So the account of a compositional context and motive and the attribution of the act of composition to some individual that are provided for in *kotobagaki* do more than make the poem and its creation an historical event; they also enhance the *aware* aspect of the experience of reading the poem by suggesting that it is a record of a recollectable, memorable experience, perhaps fleeting or even mundane but significant enough for the poet to have moved him or her to compose the poem, through which the reader can even now recollect the sentiments or sensations of that moment. A recollected sense of the historical moment of composition, the compositional motive, and the relationship of the poem to a persona and to that persona's experience are all loaded into the reading of the poem as soon as the *kotobagaki* has been read, and it is thus that it intercedes between the reader and the poem to shape the reading of the poem. For Kigin and Norinaga, the *kotobagaki* to the "*omoedomo*" poem interceded in a way that determined in great part the way that they commented on it. Their commentaries, of course, reflected the way that they read not just the poem but the *kotobagaki*, the poet's name, and the poem together as one historico-literary unit.

Documentation of the moment, motive for, and agent of composition is also the function of many of the *kotobagaki* written into the so-called *shikashū*, the comprehensive collections of the works of individual poets or groups of poets associated with certain individuals. In some of the *shikashū* the *kotobagaki* and poems can be read sequentially as chronicles of series of events across a span of time, with the poems composed in response to those events; thus, the poems are presented as lyrical responses to the events recorded historically in the *kotobagaki*. In some "group" *shikashū*, the *kotobagaki* and the series of poet's names that follow them, along with their poems, allow the reader to sense that he or she is recollecting a set of lyrical responses to a given circumstance experienced by multiple personae. The compositional act thus recorded is a collective one, a social phenomenon, and the nostalgia evoked by the reading of such sets of poems arises from the sharing of an experience that is not just two-dimensional, between poet and reader, but three-dimensional, between the composer of a single poem, the group of poets who all composed poems in the same circumstances, and the reader, who is witness to the record of that experience. Of the three *shikashū* associated with Senshi, two are collective, while the third, *Hosshin wakashū*, appears to be entirely of her own composition but addresses a collective readership.[18]

---

18. Texts of all three collections—*Daisaiin saki no gyoshū, Daisaiin gyoshū* and *HSWKS*—may be found in *SKT* 3, 279–92.

The "*omoedomo*" poem, however, is not to be found in any of the three *shikashū* to which Senshi is a major contributor, so there is not even this means for corroborating the historical/situational context that has been provided for it in the *Shika wakashū kotobagaki*. Although the poem appears nowhere earlier than in *Shika wakashū*, a work compiled over a century after Senshi's death, that does not necessarily mean that Akisuke was the author of the *kotobagaki*, but it does appear that he or some other collector or editor of poems felt it appropriate to append this explanatory note in order to help the reader make one particular kind of reading of the poem. We have seen the effect of this on Kigin and Norinaga: it gave them a key to the problems of the poem, but left certain questions for them to clarify, and in so doing they drew a picture of the poet's state of mind at the time of composition that is, in its concreteness, almost more potent than the poem alone can be. What emerges, through the combined agency of *kotobagaki*, poem, and commentary, is an image of a woman overwhelmed by internal conflict, torn between her responsibilities to one religious institution and her inclination to devote herself to another. This may be an accurate image, though perhaps a bit too highly colored. But what the Kigin and Norinaga commentaries overlook, in their search for a fuller understanding of the poem through a sense of its historical and situational context and their inevitable drive toward the personification of the poet through the agency of the poem, is the poetic character of the poem itself.

This has also been the tendency in modern analysis of Senshi's other Buddhist poems, the poems for which she is best known, and particularly in discussions of her unique cycle, *Hosshin wakashū*. In it, Senshi's poems can at least potentially be read as one imagines she intended them to be read, for her presentation of them would seem not to have been altered in any significant way by later editors or *kotobagaki* authors. But there is a preface, ostensibly by Senshi herself, to be read as one might read a *kotobagaki* for an understanding of the poet's attitude toward her work, her purpose in creating it, and some of the circumstances of its composition; and, alongside each of the fifty-five poems in the cycle, where *kotobagaki* might otherwise be found, there are instead fifty-five passages from Buddhist scripture, serving as topic-lines (*dai*), each one the basis or point of reference for the poem that follows it. The problems involved in reading and understanding this work overlap in certain ways with those encountered in reading and understanding the "*omoedomo*" poem: again, there is a special kind of compositional moment and motive that at least partially explains itself, language both conventional and unconventional to poetry to be accounted for, and a realm of subject and image not central to the *waka* tradition, though certainly a part of it. But there is also the relationship of the two kinds of text—the Buddhist passages, recorded in Chinese, and the poem-texts, in metrical Japanese, written in mixed script—to be puzzled out. The relationship of each scriptural text to each poem-text is partially analogous to the relationship between *kotobagaki* in anthologies (particularly those that simply name the topic) and the poems they introduce: in both cases, two different kinds of text, inscribed for different purposes, are paired and presented to be read as interacting segments of independent units arranged to be read in a series of such units. In *Hosshin wakashū*, however, the two texts are perhaps more structurally independent than they are in most *kotobagaki* and *waka* pairs, since the quotations from Buddhist scripture and the poems are not bound by any sort of syntactic links between them.[19] And the combined impact of topic-text and poem in *Hosshin wakashū* is also something very different from the historical, personifying, contextualizing effect of *kotobagaki*-and-poem units in the anthologies. In *Hosshin wakashū*, Senshi explored the effects of the combination of particular kinds of texts as part of a creative exercise for which she claimed (explicitly in the preface, implicitly in the poems themselves) still other goals—religious goals, to be sure, but goals that were by no means divorced from her literary concerns. One effect of this combination of two kinds of text is the suggestion of a kind of dialogue between them, or rather, a series of dialogues in which several voices participate.[20] These voices are encountered successively by the reader as the cycle of poems unfolds and the poet formulates a response to each in yet another voice, that of the "poem-speaker." The effect is analogous to that achieved by the reading of a series of poems on the same topic or related topics presented as the work of different poets in the selective anthologies; here, however, the reader understands that a single poet is the manipulator of the poem-speaker's voice, shifting it from position to position as her reading and interpretation of the succession of

---

19. Many *kotobagaki* that identify the topic of a given poem end with the attributive "X o yomeru," indicating that "what follows is a poem written [when so-and-so composed it] on the topic 'X.'" In many *kotobagaki* and other prose narrative introductions to all manner of poems, a pattern like "Y *ni yomeru*" is employed to indicate various aspects of the circumstances (place, time, social situation) of composition, or a cause and effect relationship between conditions described and poem yielded is indicated by a definite conditional, such as "Z o mireba" ("when he/she saw 'Z'") or "A o kikeba" ("when he/she heard 'A'").

20. One aspect of these dialogues that cannot be sufficiently explored here is their aural character, that is, the ways in which the sounds produced by an oral reading of the scriptural passages (in Sino-Japanese) may be responded to, imitated, or contrasted in the sounds produced by an oral reading of the poems paired with them. If enough were known about the precise manner of pronunciation of such scriptural texts by Heian readers, their aural character could be compared with the phonological characteristics of the poems. Roy Andrew Miller has called for such analyses of aural patterns in *waka* studies (see his review article, "No Time for Literature," *Journal of the American Oriental Society* 107.4 [October-December 1987]: 745–60), but no such studies have appeared as of this writing.

topic-texts shifts and turns, often finding ways to suggest that more than one kind of voice could be "speaking" a given poem. The poem-speaker frequently does voice sentiments that we can identify with Senshi, as we think we know her, but the poem-speaker's voice is really a voice that Senshi creates, or recreates, in each poem, casting it in various roles as the manner of her response to each passage takes shape. Most marked among these shifts are those from grave doubts about the speaker's capacity to attain salvation, to certainty that she will, and then again to doubt. Such vacillation may have plagued the real Senshi, but in the cycle it is imposed upon and expressed by the poem-speaker—an anonymous, though in some poems not a genderless, identity—who, moreover, expresses her vacillations and other sentiments variously as reiteration, reinterpretation, or, in some cases, as challenge to the voice or voices in the scriptural passages. None of the poems is simply a translation from the Chinese to the Japanese: in each, something has been added, emphasized, shifted, recast, or redirected, so that while each poem appears to have been crafted to display its links to its topic-text, each one emerges from that text to stand alongside it as a wholly new and decidedly different utterance.

For these and other reasons, an encounter with the cycle of Buddhist poems in *Hosshin wakashū*, while raising many of the same questions, is very different from an encounter with the "*omoedomo*" poem as presented in the *Zakki* by mid-Tokugawa shrine officials or as Kigin and Norinaga encountered it in its *Shika wakashū* setting. There, those readers read the poem as the utterance of one voice, which they could not think of as that of anyone but Senshi's, and they reacted to the poem accordingly. In *Hosshin wakashū*, the reader confronts a complex text in which multiple voices engage in a constantly shifting discourse. The challenge to the reader is to trace the ways that the poet, Senshi, shaped that discourse, using the language and rhetorical conventions of *waka* to form "new" utterances that interact with the utterances she took or received from scripture. What we know about her—particularly, what we can learn about her as a poet—helps meet that challenge, but it is the text itself that says the most about itself.

The *Zakki* introduction and the *Shika wakashū kotobagaki* to the "*omoedomo*" poem inevitably direct consideration of the poem's literary character to questions about the poet herself—her social and official position, her state of mind, the meaning of the utterance that she is supposed to have made when she faced toward the west and away from her responsibilities as Kamo priestess. Pondering these things gives a certain kind of depth to the understanding of the poem derived thereby, but it is an understanding that depends largely on the consideration of matters that are extraneous to the poem. Kigin's and Norinaga's commentaries, which do focus on the words *imu to te* in the poem, and the *Zakki* introduction, which addresses the same problem, all inevitably direct a reader to the consideration of extrapoetic matters. Perhaps such tendencies in commentary on certain poems are inescapable; indeed, there is surely no reason to erase all consideration of a poet's circumstances and motives from an analysis of that poet's poetry—at least not in cases where something about those circumstances and motives can be described with some accuracy. (Of course this is not always the case.) But the consideration of the literary character of a poem or group of poems should not stop there. There needs to be, at the same time, a consideration of the poem or poems themselves, not only as historical artifacts but as complex works in which language has been used in special ways to produce special literary effects. A real woman, with motives and goals of which she was highly conscious, wrote *Hosshin wakashū,* and no discussion of that work can ignore this woman and the motives she had for writing it. But such knowledge of her circumstances and motives as we may be able to obtain will be most useful if it helps us to understand Senshi's Buddhist poems as literary works—to deepen our understanding of her use of the language of poetry—rather than as elements of what can only be a fragmentary reconstruction of her biography.

Daughter, sister, and aunt of emperors, the imperial princess Senshi (964–1035) served for fifty-seven years, through five reigns, as High Priestess of the Kamo Shrine (*Saiin*). The Heian populace came to know her as the gracious and stately personage who appeared year after year as the chief officiant of the annual Kamo festivals, while in royal and aristocratic circles she was recognized as the centerpiece of a literary salon that was at least as prestigious as those headed by the most powerful women of the imperial court. She came to be known as *Daisaiin,* "the Great Kamo Priestess," but her public and private expressions of faith in Buddhism were as well known and as highly praised as was her long service at the shrine of the native gods. The late Heian- or early Kamakura-period author of a story about her, which is to be found in the collection of historical and semihistorical tales known as the *Kohon setsuwa shū,* wrote, "Though Buddhism was taboo for the Ise and Kamo priestesses, this *Saiin* revered Buddhism, and it was reported that she prayed and chanted every morning without fail and intoned the *Lotus Sutra* before an image of Amida all day long."[21] *Ōkagami* and other sources relate that in the very midst of the Kamo festivities she directly addressed the viewing multitudes, encouraging one and all to strive together with her for Buddhahood ("*Sanagara tomo*

---

21. Kawaguchi Hisao, ed., *Kohon setsuwa shū* (Nihon koten zensho) (Tokyo: Asahi Shinbunsha, 1967), 83–89.

ni hotoke to naramu").[22] And, in the cycle of poems composed in the autumn of 1012, which she called *Hosshin wakashū* ("A Collection of Japanese Poems for the Awakening of Faith"), she transformed a series of passages selected from the texts of Buddhist scripture into expressions of her own desire, and that of other women, for salvation.

She seems to have done so in the belief that the act of creating such poems—the application of the skills she had learned through the study and practice of secular verse to the composition of a devotional work—was the most meaningful demonstration of piety that she could make. The preface to *Hosshin wakashū* offers an explicit (and rather conventional) prayer, ostensibly Senshi's own, that the merit earned through this creative act of devotion may be shared by all those who might read the work, which would offer them the revered words of scriptures together with original poems expressing the poet's understanding of and reaction to those words. It was perfectly fitting that the language and forms of secular poetry should become Senshi's vehicle for this endeavor, for it was to the cultivation of that language that she and the women who lived with her in the Kamo priestess's official residence at Murasakino devoted much of their energies. She trained them, and trained herself, in the use of that language as an intense means for communicating among themselves and for sharing their sensibilities with the world outside the Saiin precincts; her use of that same language in the poems of *Hosshin wakashū* showed that the act of creating it was part of, not separate from, her other acts of poem making and poem sharing.

Over five hundred of the poems that Senshi and the women who lived with her at Murasakino wrote—examples of the kind of literary activity that established the Saiin's reputation for elegance and refinement, but only a fraction of the many thousands of poems that must have been written during Senshi's residence there—are preserved in two collections, *Daisaiin saki no gyoshū* and *Daisaiin gyoshū*, which include poems from 984–86 and 1014–19, respectively.[23] The informal chronologies and compositional pretexts and contexts established by the *kotobagaki* in these

22. Matsumura Hiroji, ed., *Ōkagami* (NKBT 21), 123; see also Helen Craig McCullough, trans., *Ōkagami, the Great Mirror: Fujiwara Michinaga (966–1027) and His Times* (Princeton: Princeton University Press, and Tokyo: University of Tokyo Press, 1980), 132.

23. *SKT* 3, 279–92. See also Akiba Yasutarō, Suzuki Tomotarō, and Kishigami Shinji, "Daisaiin saki no gyoshū no kenkyū" in *Nihon Daigaku sōritsu shichijūnen kinen ronbunshū*, vol. 1: *Jinbun kagaku hen* (Tokyo: Nihon Daigaku, 1960), 433–579; Hashimoto Fumio, "Daisaiin gyoshū no seikaku" in his *Ōchō waka shi no kenkyū* (Tokyo: Kasama Shoin, 1972), 419–39; Kawade Kiyohiko, "Saiinnai no seikatsu o shinobu," *Shintō shi kenkyū* 16.1 (1968): 26–46; Sasaki Takiko, "Daisaiin Senshi Naishinnō no waka" in Hokkaidō Daigaku Setsuwa Bungaku Kenkyūkai, ed., *Chūsei setsuwa no sekai* (Tokyo:

two collections make it possible to read these, like some other *shikashū*, as "poetic diaries" of these two periods. They also show how Senshi and her companions went about the writing of poetry, composing in a whole gamut of modes and moods, employing a range of strategies to suit such opportunities for poem making as might present themselves: ritual occasions, visits and communications from distinguished personages of the court and personal friends, partings and homecomings, and many instances in which the composing of poems was an almost spontaneous reaction to minute seasonal changes in the Saiin environment. On most such occasions, more than one person, often including Senshi herself, took part in the poem making, and the comparison of their poems among themselves, and the discussion of the merits or faults of each composition, must have filled many of the days and nights that these women spent in the Murasakino mansion, waiting patiently for the months to pass between the Kamo festivals.

The lexical and rhetorical range of the poems these women produced is, as may be expected, rather comparable to the range of the poetry in the *Kokin wakashū* and the subsequent anthologies that adhered closely to its standards[24]; and it will come as no surprise to find that the poems in *Hosshin wakashū* also employ essentially that same vocabulary (except, and it is an important exception, where new language is introduced into the discourse from the scriptural topic-texts), exercise the same rhetorical repertoire, and depend on the same shared understanding of what certain elements of the symbolic language of *waka* meant and how those elements should be used in *waka*. It was this kind of poem making, thoroughly ensconced within its tradition and conscious of being part of it, of which Senshi was regarded as a master; it was this that she practiced, in all her compositions, including *Hosshin wakashū*, and it was this that she shared with her protégées, in that particular work as in all her others.

A few samples from the Saiin collections may provide a good illustration of the kind of art cultivated by the Saiin poets, and will prepare us to

---

Kasama Shoin, 1979), 231–56; Naka Shūko, "Josei saron ni okeru shizen to waka: Daisaiin saron o chūshin ni" in Katagiri Yōichi, ed., *Ōchō waka no sekai: shizen kanjō to biishiki* (Tokyo: Sekai Shisōsha, 1984), 60–75; and Tokoro Kyōko, "Senshi Naishinnō Saiin kankei no wakashūsei," *Shintōshi kenkyū* 35.2 (April 1987): 61–83.

24. Naka, ibid., analyzes nature imagery in the poems in the two Saiin collections as essentially consonant with the use of that same imagery in the *Kokin wakashū*, and Motofusa Naoko has found a very large number of poems in the collections that replicate the diction and other formal characteristics of *Kokin wakashū* poems, in "Daisaiin saron no kashū ni okeru *Kokinshū* no eikyō," *Heian bungaku kenkyū* 64 (December 1980): 45–66.

see how closely the poems in *Hosshin wakashū* are linked to those traditions of secular verse that governed their activities in other compositional
settings. The *kotobagaki* of poem 39 in *Daisaiin gyoshū* introduces it as one
Senshi sent to an absent attendant, "Kodaifu," on a night when a bright
moon was intermittently obscured by clouds (*tsuki no kumorimi harezumi
suru hodo ni*), and hence unable to fulfill its most conventional *waka* role,
that of nocturnal companion:

> kumogakure sayaka ni mienu tsuki kage ni
> machimi matazumi hito zo koishiki[25]

The moon obscured by clouds (*kumogakure . . .*) sheds a light (*tsuki kage*)
that barely allows the poem-speaker to see into the night (*sayaka ni mienu*,
"I cannot see it [the moon] clearly"); nevertheless, she peers into the
darkness, waiting for the reappearance of the moon from behind the
clouds, then giving up in impatience, then looking out in hope again
(*machimi matazumi*, "waiting, then not waiting"). Similarly, she waits anx-
iously for the return of the absent Kodaifu, yearning for her companionship (*hito zo koishiki*) as much as or perhaps even more than for that of
the unhelpful moon. The juxtaposition of a similar construction in the
kotobagaki (*kumorimi harezumi*, "the moon clouding over, and not clearing")
in the setting of the scene accentuates the sense of the discomfiture of the
moment and the reflexive relationship between the moon, here a failed
companion, and Kodaifu, an absent one. The language of this poem
overtly imitates that of a poem attributed to Hitomaro in *Shūi wakashū*—

> mikazuki no sayaka ni miezu
> kumogakure mimakuzohoshiki utate kono goro[26]
> I cannot see the crescent moon clearly,
>   for it is hidden in the clouds, and I do so wish to see it;
>   what a trying time this is!

—but it is also allied with countless poems in which the obscured moon
represents a deceased or otherwise absent sovereign or other beloved
person for whom the poem-speaker pines, as in Ariwara Narihira's alle-
gorical poem (said to have been composed on a hunting expedition when
his sovereign retired early in the evening)—

---

25. *SKT* 3, 289. The poem also appears as a "miscellaneous" poem in *Gyokuyō wakashū*
(no. 2492), with a slightly revised *kotobagaki* (*SKT* 1, 474).

26. *SKT* 1, 81.

> akanaku ni madaki mo tsuki no kakururu ka
> yama no ha nigete irezu mo aranamu[27]
> The moon hides so soon, before we have seen enough of it?
> Let the peaks retreat and refuse to let it sink behind them!

—in which it is the mountains on the horizon (rather than clouds) that block the view of the yearned-for "companion." In *Hosshin wakashū* no. 12, prompted by a scriptural text on "inviting the Buddhas to remain in this world," Senshi pleads with another symbolic moon "not to hide itself amidst the clouds" (*kumogakuresede*) but to continue to shed its light on those who look up to it. (Here, "*kumogakuru*" reverberates with another of its meanings, "to die" [particularly of exalted personages, such as sovereigns, as well as loved ones].)

On another night, one on which the full moon shone in all its splendor (*tsuki no kumanaki akaki ni*), another absent attendant, "Taifu," was sent this poem by her colleague "Ukon" (*Daisaiin gyoshū* no. 121; the poem also appears as an autumn poem in *Fūga wakashū* [599], where it is attributed to Senshi)—

> kokoro sumu aki no tsuki dani nakariseba
> nani o ukiyo no nagusame ni semu[28]
> Were there not at least this autumn moon that calms the heart,
> what would be my solace in this sad life?

—a suggestion that, in Taifu's absence, the luminous moon will serve amply as substitute and solacing companion. This poem employs a rhetorical structure much like Narihira's famed

> yo no naka ni taete sakura no nakariseba
> haru no kokoro wa nodokekaramashi[29]
> Were there no cherry blossoms in this world,
> how calm springtime hearts would be!

as does *Hosshin wakashū* poem 33. Taifu's response (*Daisaiin gyoshū* no. 122) to Ukon is a claim to the same moon as her own substitute companion:

---

27. *Kokin wakashū* no. 884; *Ise monogatari* section 82.

28. *SKT* 1, 566.

29. *Kokin wakashū* no. 53.

> *kaze ni sou mugura no toko no hitorine mo*
>   *tsuki yori hoka no nagusame zo naki*
> For one who sleeps alone on a windblown pallet of grass,
>   there is no solace other than the moon.

The unmistakably erotic subtext of this exchange is part of its poetic character: the two women are playing with images and sentiments that, in another context, would readily be read as explicit tropes of sexual desire—and in *Hosshin wakashū*, those same tropes are transferred to poems expressing the poet's desire for "light" from a Buddha whose guidance and companionship she passionately craves.

In *Daisaiin saki no gyoshū* (nos. 316–22), still another moonlit night is the setting for a whole series of poems exchanged between some Saiin women and some male intruders from the outer world, and once more the moon becomes the focus of their interplay. A certain captain, visiting these precincts secretly (*shinoburu Chūjō*) tries to get the attention of the ladies inside the mansion with another mimicking of Narihira's "*yo no naka ni . . .*,"

> *naka naka ni koyoi no tsuki no nakariseba*
>   If there were no such moon as this tonight . . .,

to which one "Shin" rejoins from within,

> *sora ni kokoro no ukabamashiya*
>   would my heart be floating up there in the sky?

—that is, "My heart has gone aloft to be with the moon, but perhaps there is someone else who seeks my company tonight!" The banter initiated by this exchange continues in verse until the somber bell of the nearby Urin'in monastery interrupts, whereupon the Captain soberly intones,

> *sayo fukete kaze ni tagueru kane no oto wa*
>   *mono omou hito no mi ni zo shimikeru*
> The night deepens, and the sound of the bell carried on the
>   wind
>   sinks into the very body of this man who is deep in his
>   own thoughts.

at which point the bell is proposed as the topic for still more poems, and both visitors and visited respond to the call.[30] Here we see yet another of

---

30. I am indebted to Robert N. Huey for his suggestions concerning the English rendering of this and the preceding poem.

the strategies the Saiin denizens employed in their gentle games of poetry, the very common one of composing on preselected topics (*daiei*).[31]
Elsewhere in *Daisaiin saki no gyoshū* we see Senshi asking her companions
to compose poems on the exceptional appearance of the moon when it
shines briefly through a gap in the clouds on a rainy night (no. 116), or,
during a *Kōshin* vigil, on the softness of autumn moonlight in a cloudless
sky (nos. 365–66).[32] On another occasion (nos. 330–32) she assigns the
task of embedding a certain word—a conventional practice, producing
poems of the kind classified as *mono no na* ("names of things") in the
selective anthologies—but the word to be embedded is *kitsune* ("fox"), a
word and topic rarely encountered in the canons of Japanese verse.
Daisaiin saki no gyoshū also has poems on such unconventional topics as
"the crying of the *makuramushi*" ("pillow bug"?, nos. 181–85) and a long
series on the rare sight of tubs, called both *yubune* and *amabune* (the latter
also suggesting "a fisherman's boat" as well as "a nun's boat"), set out to
catch rain when it leaks through the roof of the Murasakino mansion (nos.
158–68).

   Hosshin wakashū is obviously a special variant of this kind of topical
composition, but in that instance Senshi set her topics for herself by
selecting (or having someone select for her) a series of passages from the
Chinese translations of the Buddhist scriptures. The fifty-five poems in
Hosshin wakashū thus are examples of *kudai*, composition on quotations
(especially quotations in Chinese), another conventional mode that is itself a variant of *daiei*. In Ōe Chisato's *Kudai waka* (also known as *Chisato
shū*), the earliest example of a collection of Japanese *kudai* poems (composed in 894 or 897), the *ku* (quoted lines of poetry) that constitute the *dai*

---

31. On the origins and development of *daiei* in *waka*, see Ozawa Masao, "Daiei kō" in his
    Kokinshū no sekai (Tokyo: Hanawa Shobō, 1961), 219–46.

32. On a Kōshin night, various entertainments—including collective poetry composition
    and other games—were devised in order to help the participants stay awake until
    dawn and thus to prevent the "three worms" (*sanshi*) believed to reside within the
    body from escaping while one slept. Were they to escape, they might report one's evil
    deeds to the celestial gods of judgment, as a result of which one's life span might be
    drastically shortened. For a study of Kōshin beliefs and cults, see Kubo Noritada,
    Kōshin shinkō (Tokyo: Yamakawa Shuppansha, 1956, reprinted 1971).
       Using *kotobagaki* and poems from *Daisaiin gyoshū* and other *shikashū*, Hagitani Boku
    has reconstructed four *utaawase* held at the Saiin at various times during Senshi's
    residence, three of which appear to have derived their central topic (*dai*) from a
    concurrent object-contest (*mono awase*): in the Kanna era (985–87) there was a "firefly
    contest" (*hotaru awase*) and an "insect contest" (*makewaza mushi awase*) during a Kōshin
    vigil in the eighth month, and in the seventh month of 1017 there was a "grass
    contest" (*kusa awase*). See Hagitani Boku, ed., *Heianchō utaawase taisei*, 10 vols. (Kyoto:
    Dōmeisha, reprinted 1979), vol. 2, 625–26, and vol. 3, 745–46.

are all from secular Chinese poems (by Bai Juyi and others).[33] There are examples of *kudai* poems in several other anthologies which suggest that this was a favored device whereby the topics of certain poetry matches (*utaawase*) were set.[34] *Wakan rōeishū,* compiled in 1018 by Fujiwara Kintō (966–1041) is a collection of poems and parts of poems, both Chinese and Japanese, familiar at that time and frequently chanted to musical tunes, but its classification system, which groups pairs and series of "songs" as variations on given topics and on one another, also must have made it useful as a kind of handbook of topical composition in conventional modes and of *kudai* composition in particular.

Hosshin wakashū is an extended exercise in *kudai* composition engaged in neither playfully nor competitively but as a professed act of devotion. Its seriousness is established in its preface and is sustained throughout the cycle, lightened occasionally when Senshi senses the potential for amusing play between her scriptural topic-texts and her own poems. Most of the passages selected as topics for *Hosshin wakashū* are from verse-passages in the scriptures, but a few are prose. Among the topic-passages are twenty-eight from each of the chapters of the *Lotus Sutra*—the text to which she was reported to have been so particularly devoted—and Senshi's twenty-eight poems on them are among the earliest known examples of this particular form of devotion to that text. Fujiwara Kintō and the poetess known as Akazome Emon (active 957 or 964–1041) are two contemporaries of Senshi's who also wrote sets of verses on passages from each chapter of the *Lotus,* called *nijūhappon no uta,* which survive intact.[35] Kintō's set is believed to have been composed in about 1002, as one of several sets commissioned by Senshi's powerful cousin Fujiwara Michinaga (966–1027) in connection with memorial services for his late sister, the dowager empress Higashi Sanjōin. In a preface to these sets of *nijūhappon no uta,* Fujiwara Arikuni (943–1011) named the Nara monk Gyōki (688–749) and the *Kokinshū* poets Henjō (816–90) and Sosei (fl. ca. 859–963), also monks, as forerunners in a tradition linking Buddhism and *waka,* but he noted that "no one has as yet used the *Lotus Sutra* as topic-

---

33. See *SKT* 3, 146–48.

34. See Ozawa, "Kudai shi to kudai waka," *Kokugo to kokubungaku* 29.11 (November 1952): 9–20; Helen Craig McCullough, *Brocade by Night: Kokin wakashū and the Court Style in Japanese Court Poetry* (Stanford: Stanford University Press, 1985), 254–61.

35. In *SKT* 3, 305–6, 322–26. The poems are preceded by the titles of the chapters of the *Lotus Sutra,* as *dai;* the specific passages alluded to are not reproduced, as they are in *HSWKS.*

texts (*imada Hokekyō o motte dai to seshi mono wa arazaru nari*)."[36] Thus, Arikuni declares the sets composed by Kintō and his peers—the others were offered by Fujiwara Tadanobu, Minamoto Toshikata, and Fujiwara Yukinari—to be the first of their kind. All four poets (known collectively as the "Four Counselors" of the court of Emperor Ichijō and admired for their literary and administrative skills[37]) were, as Arikuni noted, longtime retainers as well as relatives of the late empress and her brother.[38] Akazome Emon was also in Michinaga's family service. So Senshi's own *nijūhappon no uta* series in *Hosshin wakashū* appears to be an example of a devotional literary form invented by others in her proximate social sphere not long before she herself adopted it.[39]

Her twenty-eight *Lotus* poems, however, are framed by additional poems on the so-called "opening" and "closing" sutras (the *Muryōgikyō* and the *Kanfugengyō*) of the *Lotus* triad (*Hokke sanbukyō*[40]) and are embedded within a compositional project of still larger proportions, in which many other scriptural sources are drawn upon in a parallel manner. In each of these fifty-five encounters between scriptural and *waka* texts we see part of a process of appropriation of *waka* diction, rhetoric, and symbol systems into religiously oriented contexts, as well as the incorporation of new or newly recast motifs and topoi introduced from the scriptural texts

---

36. "Hokekyō nijūhappon o sansuru waka no jo" in *Honchō monzui* 11. See Kakimura Shigematsu, ed., *Honchō monzui chūshaku* 2 (Tokyo: Fuzanbō, 1922, reprinted 1968), 608. According to attributions in a number of later anthologies, one important predecessor or contemporary of Kintō et al. in *nijūhappon no uta* composition was the famous priest Genshin (942–1017); see Fujii Chikai, *Ōjōyōshū no bunkashiteki kenkyū* (Kyoto: Heiraku Shoten, 1978), 216–30.

37. See William H. McCullough and Helen C. McCullough, trans., *A Tale of Flowering Fortunes: Annals of Japanese Aristocratic Life in the Heian Period,* 2 vols. (Stanford: Stanford University Press, 1980), 169n.

38. Tadanobu and Yukinari were Michinaga's first cousins, and Toshikata was the brother of one of his wives.

39. Takagi Yutaka, *Heian jidai hokke bukkyō shi no kenkyū* (Kyoto: Heirakuji Shoten, 1973), 260–63. See also Yamada Shōzen, "Poetry and Meaning: Medieval Poets and the *Lotus Sutra*," in George J. Tanabe, Jr., and Willa Jane Tanabe, eds., *The Lotus Sutra in Japanese Culture* (Honolulu: University of Hawaii Press, 1989), 95–117. Yamada vehemently asserts that the emergence of *nijūhappon no uta* was dependent on earlier instances of composition of Chinese poems on *Lotus Sutra* excerpts by men, to whom he refers (quite noxiously) as "the standard bearers of culture" (101).

40. The association of the three sutras as a group is very early, probably predating Zhihyi, or so his traditional biographies would suggest. See *Sui T'ien-t'ai Zhi-zhe Da-shi biechuan* (*T* no. 2050) in Takakusu Junjirō and Watanabe Kaigyoku, eds., *Taishō shinshū daizōkyō*, 85 vols. (Tokyo: Taishō Issaikyō Kankōkai, 1924–32), vol. 50, 191c. Hereafter this work will be cited as *T*.

into the *waka* lexicon.[41] The Buddhist scriptures to which Senshi turned her attention are extremely rich in figural and decorative language, tending particularly to floral and aquatic imagery that, as it happens, is frequently analogous to and easily assimilated in the conventional image systems of *waka*. Simile and metaphor are fundamental elements of scriptural rhetoric, as are hyperbole, pattern repetition, and, of course, parallelism, and this is particularly so in verse-passages (*gāthā*), from which, not surprisingly, most of the *Hosshin wakashū* topic-passages are taken and which, thus extracted, provide much that can be readily imitated or reflected in the *waka* made to stand beside them. Some of these features were already organic elements of *waka*, but the special compositional situation that Senshi created for herself in undertaking the *Hosshin wakashū* project also allowed her to test the ways that the language of scripture might act upon the style and substance of her own verse.

Hosshin wakashū has been deemed the earliest independent collection of *Shakkyōka* ("poems on the teachings of the Buddha") by a single poet— in contrast to the "Buddhist poems" selected from the works of various poets found in groups in some anthologies—by those who have considered its devotional nature and its *kudai* form as hallmarks of that genre, most descriptions of which de-emphasize the relationship that such poems may bear to those in the corpus that are not so labeled.[42] The classifying label "*Shakkyōka*" was first employed as a subsection title in the miscellaneous section of *Goshūi wakashū*, the fourth imperial collection of poetry, compiled in the latter half of the eleventh century (1075–86).[43]

---

41. In the analysis of the *HSWKS* poems that follows, we shall pay special attention to the ways that Senshi handles such elements of the *waka* lexicon as the poetic language of "meeting" (various forms of the verb *au*, in nos. 16, 26, 32, 35, 49, 51, and 52); "seeing" (*miru, miyu,* in nos. 18, 20, 40, and 41); and "seeking" (*tazunu, motomu,* in nos. 24, 25, and 31); the significances of "dream" (*yume,* in nos. 13, 25, 50) and of such old forms as the *makurakotoba* "*kagerō no*" (no. 42); and the symbolism of falling flowers (no. 41) and the seasonal and other associations of the imagery of "dew" (*tsuyu,* in nos. 28, 30, and 53), as occasions for their use are prompted by various elements of the scriptural topic-texts. We shall also see how some of those texts tested her ingenuity as poemmaker with their presentation of such special (and not inherently *waka*-like) topics as the obstructions that bar women from Buddhahood and the related idea of gender transformation (nos. 1, 2, 16, 36, 47, 48), and how she is prompted by those texts to manipulate such ubiquitous and potent *waka* images as the moon (*tsuki*) and the traveler's path (*michi*) in specific ways.

42. This is the case with Ishihara Kiyoshi's *Shakkyōka no kenkyū* (Kyoto: Dōmeisha, 1980), which is nevertheless an extremely useful study of a large number of poems. Ishihara limits his discussion of *Shakkyōka* to poems so classified in the *chokusenshū,* an approach that sidesteps the issue of what does or does not distinguish these poems from other *waka* other than the fact that they have been thus classified by anthologizers.

43. See Morrell, "The Buddhist Poetry in the *Goshūishū*," 89–90.

Then, beginning with the *Senzai wakashū*, the seventh anthology, compiled in 1183–87, *Shakkyōka* were alotted a separate section in most subsequent anthologies.[44] The designation "*Shakkyōka*" was and has been applied to almost any poem that has anything to do with Buddhism, so it labels many poems that, were it not for this particular topical aspect or the presence of a distinctly Buddhist word or image, would not otherwise be distinguished as any sort of special group. What we may call "*kudai Shakkyōka*"—*kudai* poems that take Buddhist scriptural passages as their topics—are to be found among the *Shakkyōka* selected for inclusion in most of the anthologies with *Shakkyōka* sections, alongside other "Buddhist poems" that refer or allude obliquely to Buddhist doctrines, practices, or personalities but do not necessarily make direct allusion to any scriptural text either in their *kotobagaki* or in the words of the poem itself. Usually, something in the *kotobagaki* provided for each *Shakkyōka* poem, whether in a section of an anthology so labeled or not, makes clear what its relevance to the religion may be. Many, for example, say that the poem is composed on the subject (*dai*) defined as "the essential purport" or "underlying sentiment" (*kokoro*) of such and such a sutra, or a specific section or passage therein.[45] Composition of such a verse might well follow upon the poet's own recitation or silent reading of the scripture or a specific part of it, or in the aftermath of a rite during which priests or other officiants had chanted the sutra or even enacted passages in it.[46] Many poems classified

---

44. Ishihara, *Shakkyōka no kenkyū*, 11–12.

45. The *Goshūi wakashū* and the *Kin'yō wakashū* are the first imperial anthologies in which *kotobagaki* with this formulation appear. It is clear that the poems thus introduced were composed on occasions when, for one reason or another, the composer had reason to focus attention on a specific passage and then to ponder its purport as a *waka* topic. Such circumstances can often be traced (fairly reliably) in fuller diarylike *kotobagaki* for poems found in *shikashū* that also were included in *chokusenshū*. It should be noted that the topical formulation X *no kokoro o yomu* is familiar from earlier secular *waka* contexts, such as occasions when lords asked their companions to compose on "the emotional essence of [the experience of] travel" (*tabi no kokoro o yome*), as in *Ise monogatari* section 9. It might be said that this is also the implied relationship between the topic-passages and poems in HSWKS, even though the scriptural quotations are not appended with "*no kokoro o [yomeru]*," but the absence of that phrase may imply, conversely, that the relationship between topic-text and responding poem is even more intimate than "*no kokoro o*" would suggest.

46. During elaborate readings of the *Lotus Sutra* as a series of "eight lectures" (*hakkō*), for example, the "Devadatta" chapter was often dramatized with a procession in which monks carried brushwood and vessels of water, in imitation of the activities of the ancient Buddha-to-be when he was the servant of a sagacious and strict ascetic. One of the most memorable accounts of such a procession is in the "Minori" chapter of *Genji monogatari*, where the performance prompts the composition of several poems by Murasaki, the sponsor of the rite, and the other senior ladies of Genji's establishment who witness it with her.

as *Shakkyōka* seem to be close, almost mechanical renderings of the Chinese in the Japanese Buddhist canonical texts into Japanese language and *tanka* form, but such renderings may fittingly embody the devotee/poet's wish to pay homage to what has just been read or heard by recapitulating it in a form that displays a kind of personal appropriation of its content and message. Or they may even have been conceived as substitutes for a reading of the sutras themselves when, for one reason or another (such as the exclusion of women from some religious precincts, or other social constraints) the poet/devotee could not be present at or participate in the reading, or was somehow incapable of carrying it out. Then, on the other hand, there is Izumi Shikibu's famous

> *kuraki yori kuraki michi ni zo irinubeki*
> *haruka ni terase yama no ha no tsuki*[47]
> From darkness into a still darker path I must go,
> so cast your light afar, oh moon upon the mountain ridge.

first anthologized in the miscellaneous section of *Shūi wakashū* (poem 1342). This poem uses the words of a passage in the "Parable of the Conjured City" chapter of the *Lotus Sutra*[48] (a passage also employed as a topic-line by Senshi for poem no. 31 in *Hosshin wakashū*), but none of the versions of the *kotobagaki* attached to this poem in the various collections in which it appears (including some versions of the *Izumi Shikibu shū*) are explicit about the relationship between the source-text and Shikibu's poem. Instead, they are concerned with the description of the poem's compositional context—as part of a correspondence with the monk Shōkū of Mount Shosha in Harima. Although the *kotobagaki* do not identify this poem as a *kudai* poem as such, its relationship to the language of a particular passage in a particular scriptural text is a very important part of the way it "works" as a poem. That relationship was probably quite clear to most of those who would have read or heard the poem when Shikibu composed it and for several centuries afterward, and this perhaps made any explicit identification of the source of the reverberant "*kuraki yori kuraki michi ni zo irinubeki*" unnecessary. At any rate, the authors of *kotobagaki* for this poem apparently preferred to emphasize its character as a message from the poet to the monk; this, in turn, allows the reader to perceive that the bright moon whose companionship and cooperation is

---

47. *SKT* 1, 93.

48. *T* 9, 22c. See also Leon Hurvitz, trans., *Scripture of the Lotus Blossom of the Fine Dharma* (New York and London: Columbia University Press, 1976), 133.

sought in this poem is not only the symbol of enlightenment—as it so often is in *Shakkyōka*—but also stands for the priest in Harima, the adept from whom Shikibu seeks guidance as she makes her way through the world.[49]

Its *kudai*-like form and the double intent of its imagery help make Izumi Shikibu's "*kuraki yori*" one of the best known of all so-called "*Shakkyōka*." The imagery of the moon as enlightened being and as spiritual guide—resonating with its other roles as "companion" in secular verse—is repeatedly employed by Senshi as well, and it is clear that this is one among many figures that poets almost automatically associated with the task of composing poems on Buddhist topics. The figuration of the moon as spiritual companion in Buddhist poetry may also bear a relationship to the *mikkyō* practice of contemplating an image of the full moon (*getsurinkan* or *gachirinkan*) as a symbol of, and in order to attain, the state of full enlightenment.[50] We shall see how useful and potent these figures were for Senshi when she engaged in the task of writing a full cycle of Buddhist poems; they appear, of course, when directly suggested by the scriptural topic-texts, but also independently, and the reader senses the poet turning and returning to them as essential tools in the performance of her creative exercise.

A few of the poems that resulted from that exercise are included in the *Shakkyōka* sections of later anthologies, where their scriptural topic-lines usually serve in the place of *kotobagaki*.[51] But a reading of them as a complete cycle, together with the scriptural quotations to which they are so closely bound, is very different from a reading of one or two of them cast together with other *Shakkyōka* of various kinds. Senshi designed *Hosshin wakashū* so that it could be read as a single sustained work employing two contrasting kinds of language—two kinds of text—woven together in one fabric. All the scriptural quotations and all the poems based on them can be read in sequence, as a kind of ritual exercise, a variant, in a sense, of *tendoku* readings of scripture, in which only selected parts of a Buddhist sutra are read but with the expectation that the impact of such reading—the salutary effect or the residual merit—will be equal to that which

---

49. See Okazaki, "Izumi Shikibu to Shōkū Shōnin: 'kuraki yori' no uta o megutte" in *Heianchō joryū sakka no kenkyū*, 175–92. See also Edwin A. Cranston, "The Dark Path: Images of Longing in Japanese Love Poetry," *Harvard Journal of Asiatic Studies* 35 (1975): 60–99, especially 99.

50. See Yamada Shōzen, "Getsurinkan to chūsei waka" in Bukkyō Minzoku Gakkai, ed., *Katō Shōichi sensei koki kinen ronbunshū: Bukkyō to girei* (Tokyo: Kokusho Kankōkai, 1977), 301–14.

51. See n. 1 in part two, below, for a list of *HSWKS* poems included in later *chokusenshū*.

would come from a reading of the whole. The copying of whole sutras and groups of sutras may also be partially analogous to Senshi's idea of copying representative portions of a series of sutras and adding her own poems to them. In the autumn of 1007 (Kankō 4.8), Senshi's cousin Michinaga, then at the apogee of his brilliant political career, took a set of sutras that he himself had copied and went to Kinbusen, a holy mountain in the Yoshino district, where he had them ritually buried. The set included a complete *Lotus Sutra* along with the *Muryōgikyō, Kanfugengyō, Amidakyō, Miroku jōshōkyō* and *Miroku geshōkyō,* and the *Hannya shingyō* ("*Heart Sutra*")[52]—all of which, except for the *Miroku* (Maitreya) sutras, are among the sutras from which Senshi took quotations for *Hosshin wakashū.*

The copying and burying of scriptures were among the most conspicuous forms of text-focused devotional practice carried out or sponsored by Heian aristocrats. They also wrote, or had written for them, certain special literary works that were deemed venerable and meritorious because of their reliance on scriptural sources. Such a work, for example, was *Sanbōe,* the collection of Buddhist tales compiled in 984 by Minamoto Tamenori for the imperial princess Sonshi (Senshi's niece and her predecessor as Saiin), and it also bears some resemblance to *Hosshin wakashū* in that much of its text consists of adapted quotations or summaries of passages from other works, including in particular a large number of scriptural sources. Tamenori emphasized this aspect of *Sanbōe* in presenting it to Sonshi, who had recently taken Buddhist vows: he claimed that the writing and reading of this kind of text—and the viewing of the illustrations that were supposed to go along with it—would add to the stores of merit that would eventually lead to good rebirths for both himself and his reader. At the end of the preface to each of the three volumes of the text, Tamenori described his own gesture of reverence toward it—a pious joining together of his palms over the manuscript, indicating his high estimation of its virtues—and in poems in Chinese at the end of each volume he repeated his praise for this text that he had created by culling its contents from other praiseworthy texts.[53]

One other analogue to *Hosshin wakashū* may be seen in Tamenori's own description in *Sanbōe* 3.14 of the Kangakue ("Society for the Advancement of Learning"), an association formed in 964 by devout laymen (probably including Tamenori) and monks from the Enyrakuji monasteries who

---

52. Takagi, *Heian jidai hokke bukkyō shi no kenkyū,* 207.

53. See Koizumi Hiroshi and Takahashi Nobuyuki, eds., *Shohon taishō Sanbōe shūsei* (Tokyo: Kasama Shoin, 1980); and Edward Kamens, *The Three Jewels: A Study and Translation of Minamoto Tamenori's Sanbōe* (Michigan Monograph Series in Japanese Studies, No. 2) (Ann Arbor: Center for Japanese Studies, The University of Michigan, 1988).

met at intervals to pray, to recite the scriptures, especially the *Lotus*, and to compose poems in Chinese on topics taken from the *Lotus* and other sutras. The men who participated in the Kangakue did so, according to Tamenori, in order to find a way to use their worldly learning for spiritual ends. Quoting the famous lines from a preface to poems that Bai Juyi presented to the Xiang-shan monastery, they proclaimed their collective desire to turn the "wild words and fanciful phrases" of their secular works into hymns in praise of the Buddhist teachings, and, emulating that prayer, they wrote offertory stanzas in Chinese on passages in the scriptures that presented them with powerful images of the Pure Land.[54] It was the collective wish of this confraternity that all of its members might reach that Pure Land together, and they pledged to help one another in that endeavor.

Similarly, the preface to *Hosshin wakashū* expresses the desire to share the benefits that might accrue from the writing and reading of it—a quasi-scripture, containing both the words of the sutras and the author's own poems inspired thereby—with any and all persons who might "see or hear it, in every life and every world," with all of whom she is eager to form a spiritual bond. This sentiment was very much in keeping with the spirit of the scriptures from which she quoted, with their promises of salvation for all sentient beings. Most immediately, however, her audience would have been the women who lived with her at Murasakino, and in many ways the religious interests and experiences embodied in *Hosshin wakashū* are those that she would have shared most closely with them.

If the poems in *Daisaiin saki no gyoshū* and *Daisaiin gyoshū* are an accurate indication, Buddhism did not loom overly large among the various interests of the ladies who lived with Senshi—at least not in any way that was disproportionate with the religion's role in most of lay society. If anything, the women of the Saiin were most acutely aware that things pertaining to Buddhism were not supposed to be allowed to manifest themselves within their precincts, and especially not in their speech. Technically, the *Engi shiki* (procedural handbooks for the enforcement of legal codes, compiled during the Engi era, 901–22) only specified seven *imikotoba*—most literally, words to be abstained from—and euphemisms approved for use in the Saiin establishment. These seven, which are identical to the "outer" seven *imikotoba* specified for use in the Saigū, the residence of the High Priestess of the Ise Shrine, do not include euphemisms for any Buddhist words as such.[55] The euphemisms for the seven

---

54. See Yanai Shigeshi, "Kangakue ni okeru shakkyōshi," *Kyōritsu Daigaku Tanki Daigakubu kiyō* 7 (December 1963): 16–27.

55. *Engi shiki,* in Kuroita, ed., *Shintei zōho kokushi taikei* 14, 99 and 131.

"outer" *imikotoba* are *naoru*, for *shi* or *shinu*, "to die"; *yasumi* for *yamai*, "sickness"; *shiotare* for *naki*, "weeping"; *ase* for *chi*, "blood"; *natsu* for *utsu*, "to strike" or "wound"; *kusahira* for *niku*, "flesh"; and *tsuchikure* for *haka*, "grave" or "tomb." Obviously, all have something to do with the chief sources of pollution to sacred sanctuaries and the purity of person that shrine officials and participants in ritual had to maintain, and the euphemisms substitute positive or neutral words (*naoru* suggests "recover from illness," *yasumi* suggests "rest," *ase* is a synonym for "sweat") for their negative counterparts. Also, whereas the "outer" list replaces native Japanese words with others of their kind, the "inner" *imikotoba* list for the Saigū replaces specifically Buddhist words that are almost all either translations or transliterations of Sanskrit words, and the euphemisms appear in most cases to be words invented for just this purpose. Thus, *nakago* is designated as the euphemism for *Butsu* or *hotoke*, "Buddha"; *somekami* for *kyō*, "sutra"; *araragi* for *tō*, "reliquary" or "pagoda"; *kawarafuki* for *ji* or *tera*, "Buddhist monastery"; *kaminaga* for *sō*, "Buddhist monk"; *mekaminaga* for *ni* or *ama*, "Buddhist nun"; and *katashiki* (or *katasonae*) for *sai* or *toki*, the monastic morning meal or "vegetarian feast." (In addition, two "extra" words to be avoided [*betsu imikotoba*] and their substitutes were specified: *koritaki* for *dō*, "worship hall," and *tsunowasu* for *ubasoku*, a layman who adheres closely to the Buddhist vows.) This set of euphemisms may not be as positive or neutral as the "outer" ones are: *somekami*, suggesting "dyed paper," and *kaminaga* and *mekaminaga*, which suggest "long-hair" and "female long-hair"—the very opposite of the way that a real monk or nun would be groomed—must have had a rather derisive ring in some usages.

Most scholars assume that both the "inner" and "outer" *imikotoba* lists governed speech at the Saiin as well as at the Saigū, even though the letter of the codes does not seem to have required this. (Exceptions apparently were made to allow the use of the forbidden Buddhist words at the time of mourning for a deceased High Priestess.[56]) One does wonder how conscientiously these restrictions were observed—Norinaga's views on the "*omoedomo*" poem notwithstanding—and how such extraordinary rules of speech, if they really did require these women to say one thing when they meant another, might have affected other aspects of the language they used among themselves, both in formal and informal conversation and

---

56. Sasaki, "Daisaiin Senshi Naishinnō no waka," 243. In a study of *imikotoba* originally published in 1917, Andō Masatsugu cited Senshi's "*omoedomo*" poem, with its *Shika wakashū kotobagaki*, as evidence for the observance of the full set of prohibitions at the Saiin. He also quoted the *Kamo chūshin zakki* reference to the poem to support this interpretation. Andō Masatsugu, "Imyō ingo no kenkyū o nobete toku ni Saigū imikotoba o ronzu," in *Andō Masatsugu chosakushū 5: Nihon bunkashi ronkō* (Tokyo: Yūsankaku, 1974), 332–65.

even in their making of poems, an art that had its own peculiar codes and special valuations of specific words and usages. If the poems in the two Saiin collections can be used as evidence, it would appear that they were quite scrupulous in their observance of the strictures, for none of the forbidden words appear in their poems except the word *ama*—the only true *kago* or *utakotoba* (word included in the standard poetic lexicon) in the list—which could slip by when used for its alternate meaning of "fisherman" or "fisherwoman." A poet identified as "Onna bettō" used this common pun when the Saiin received the news that another woman, called "Koseshi," had become a nun (*ama ni narinuru yoshi kikoesasetaru*) at the end of the forty-nine days of mourning for "the former governor of Musashi"—presumably Koseshi's husband or close relative (*Daisaiin gyoshū* nos. 34–35).[57] But when "the wife of the chief of the Cavalry of the Right" informed Senshi that she was going to become a nun ("*migi no muma no kami no onna, ama ni naru to te kikoesasetaru*," says the *kotobagaki*) she initiated an exchange of poems (*Daisaiin gyoshū* nos. 27–29) in which both correspondents managed to avoid the timeworn *ama* device. The new nun's poem, a justification of her act and an announcement of her altered condition, says,

> *wagami sae arishi ni mo arazu narinikeri*
> *yo no tsunenasa o omoikoshi ma ni*
> I find that even I myself am no longer what I once was;
>> the change has come upon me even as I brooded on the
>> transience of this world.

And Senshi's reply says,

> *somukinuru utosa o sae wa omou ka na*
> *konata wa itodo yoso ni narinu to*
> I wonder if you give a thought to all the sadness from
>> which you now have turned away,
>> or sense how great has grown the gulf between us.

---

57. In *Kokin waka rokujō* book 2 there is a poem (no. 1450) attributed to "the Saiin"—probably Senshi—in which the image of a small fishing boat (*ama kobune*) becomes the focus of the poet's sense of separation:

nami nagara sode zo nurenuru
ama kobune noriokuretaru wagami zo omoeba
Amidst these waves my sleeves are soaked,
so sorry am I to think that I have not boarded the little boat that bears the fisherman/nun away.

In *SKT* 2; see also Sasaki, ibid., 243.

Like many poems on the occasion of the *shukke* (taking vows and becoming a Buddhist monk or nun) of friends and acquaintances, Senshi's poem deals with separation, distance, a sense of being left behind or excluded, and envy—sometimes, in such poems, envy tinged with a gentle reproach against the one who has "gone ahead" or self-deprecation by the one who has "remained behind." Here, the sadness (*utosa*) that the "wife of the chief of the Cavalry of the Right" has turned her back on is both the innate sadness of the mundane world—the *"yo no tsunenasa"* of the first poem—and the sadness of Senshi and the other old friends who have been left behind in that world, a world in which they already felt distanced from the Buddhist sphere that their former companion now has entered. And so they who remain behind are now separated (*yoso ni narinu*) from the new nun in a new way that only increases their sense of loss and their melancholy. The nun's reply shows her respect for these sentiments and for the tenderness of their expression:

> *kagerō no yo no tsunenasa o omoishiru*
> *hito no kokoro o shiru hito mogana*
> I wish that I had here with me a person who understands
>   the feelings of one who has understood how transient
>   this world is.

She has returned to the first poem's *"yo no tsunenasa,"* this time adding the *makurakotoba* *"kagerō no,"* which deepens the invocation of mutability[58]; the echo of *"omoishiru"* in *"hito no kokoro o shiru"* also suggests that there is still much that the two women may have in common: so, all in all, the poem compliments Senshi for the sensitivity that she has shown and thereby hints that the gulf between the two women's spiritual states may not be so great after all.

The conventions for abstinence or avoidance in language were only one manifestation of the exclusion of Buddhism from the lives of the Saiin women and of their exclusion from it. There were, of course, other restrictions that governed their behavior while in the Kamo service: when they menstruated, for example, they had to withdraw, as if quarantined, to special quarters designated the *asedono*, a euphemistic "hall for bleeding." Literary sources also indicate that the Saiin herself was forbidden to shave her hair and could not have face-to-face social intercourse with

---

58. See also the discussion of *HSWKS* poem 42 in part two, below.

persons who had taken Buddhist vows.[59] So most of the experience of Buddhism that these women could have was an experience of something that was going on in the world beyond the walls of their abode. The precise location of the Murasakino mansion is no longer known, but it was very close to the famous Urin'in, a monastery that was often favored by visitors from the imperial court, and the denizens of the Saiin were keenly aware of their comings and goings. Very late one night, according to a *kotobagaki* in *Daisaiin saki no gyoshū* (no. 223), "Muma," another of Senshi's women, was awakened by the hubbub of carriages returning to the palace after the evening's *nenbutsu* service had finally come to a close (*"Urin'in no nenbutsu ni kitaru kuruma no, yo fukuru hodo ni kikoyureba"*). Muma's poem records her thoughts as she lay awake listening to the bustle outside:

> *kumoi yori nori no kuruma zo kaeru naru*
> *nishi ni katabuku tsuki ya auramu*
> Do the carriages that brought them from on high to hear
> the dharma turn homeward now because they have had
> their encounter with the moon that is sinking in the west?

Though it is not written in a strictly devotional context, this poem contains several elements frequently seen in poems classified as *Shakkyōka*. The carriages, which come from "on high," literally "amidst the clouds" (*kumoi yori*)—that is, the court—are also *nori no kuruma*: not just "carriages on which they <u>ride</u>" (*noru*) but "carriages of <u>the dharma</u>" (*nori*)—vehicles that bear them to and from the place where they can receive and participate in the Buddhist teachings, and vehicles that evoke the carriages offered to his children by a devout Buddhist as symbols of the unity of the many forms of the religion in a famous parable in the *Lotus Sutra*. The same "*nori no kuruma*" appears in *Hosshin wakashū* (in poem 27). And once again, in the present poem, the moon seems to represent the fulfillment of the hopes held by those who have spent the evening in prayer at the Urin'in: they have been worshiping Amida, and in doing so may have achieved contact with his symbol, the moon, now declining over the western horizon, pointing the way to his Pure Land—where, Muma speculates, his worshipers are now more likely than even before to be able to join him for eternity. The poem encodes her yearning to be one with them—a desire that, for now, as a resident of the Saiin, she cannot act upon.

---

59. The "*Koromo no tama*" chapter of *Eiga monogatari* describes Senshi's emotional reunion with her half brother, Prince Munehira, who took vows in 981 and therefore could not visit her until she retired as Saiin, in 1031. Matsumura Hiroji and Yamanaka Yutaka, eds., *Eiga monotagari* 2 (NKBT 76), 384.

Senshi's own particularly acute sense of exclusion from the devotions pursued by others "outside," and of her distance and difference from them, surfaces repeatedly in her poems, to such an extent that a reading of those of her works that are included in the various *chokusenshū* may suggest that this was, for her, a dominant theme. One of its most succinct expositions is the poem that appears in the "laments" section of *Shūi wakashū* (poem 1337) with the *kotobagaki*, "Composed when she had the figure of a tortoise fashioned from gold to be sent as an offering for the Service of Eight Lectures sponsored by the Empress-Mother (*Nyoin no gohakkō ni hōmochi ni kane shite kame no kata o tsukurite yomihaberikeru*)." The sponsor of these lectures on the *Lotus Sutra* was the Saiin's sister-in-law Senshi, known as Higashi Sanjō-in, the consort of the emperor En'yū and the mother of the emperor Ichijō (the woman in whose memory, at a later date, the *nijūhappon no uta* sets described above were composed). The date of the service is uncertain, but it probably occurred between Higashi Sanjō-in's initial tonsure (*rakushoku*) in 991 and her death at the age of forty in 1001; the Saiin Senshi would have been in her late twenties or her thirties at the time.[60] The gift of the tortoise was an allusion to a well-known image in the *Lotus Sutra* itself, and so, in a more complex way, was the Saiin's poem:

> *gō tsukusu mitarashigawa no kame nareba*
> *nori no ukigi ni awanu narikeri*
> I am a tortoise that must live out my destiny in this River
> of Purification,
>   so I shall never encounter that "floating piece of wood"
>   that is the dharma.

In the *Myōshōgon bon* chapter of the *Lotus*—in a passage that Senshi also used for poem-topic 51 in *Hosshin wakashū*—it is said that "a Buddha is as hard to encounter as it would be for a one-eyed tortoise to encounter a hole in a floating piece of wood": thus, those who do encounter a Buddha who can give them the teachings of the *Lotus* must know how very fortunate they are.[61] Knowing, of course, that her sister-in-law would encounter this passage during the course of the Eight Lectures, the Saiin had

60. Sasaki, "*Daisaiin Senshi Naishinnō no waka*," 246. Tokoro Kyōko thinks the poem was written after 1001. See Tokoro Kyōko, "Saiin Senshi Naishinnō no Bukkyō shinkō," *Shintōshi kenkyū* 32.3 (July 1984): 29, 40–41.

61. For a discussion of the figure *nori no ukigi* and related figurings of the dharma (*nori*), including some, such as *nori no tomoshibi* ("the dharma torch") that are also employed in HSWKS (poem 33), see Katagiri Yōichi, *Utamakura utakotoba jiten* (Tokyo: Kadokawa Shoten, 1983), 321–22.

commisioned an artisan to prepare an offering that would symbolize it, while she herself prepared a poem in which she spoke of herself as the tortoise. But this tortoise is one whose fate in this life, decreed by the karma of the past, is to spend its long life in the "River of Purification" (Mitarashigawa) at Kamo—the stream that flowed through the Kamo Shrine precincts and in which Senshi, as Kamo priestess, periodically had to perform a ritual cleansing of her person, particularly in the days prior to the Kamo festivals. Since it is her lot, she says, to serve in this post—to have served many years, and to anticipate serving many more, going on and on through time as does the tortoise—she has not really had nor will be likely to have an opportunity to "meet" (*au*) the Buddha's teachings.[62] She would no doubt have wished to attend the *Hakkō* herself, or to have sponsored one of her own, if only she could have. Thus, the poem she wrote on this occasion can be read as a frank expression of the resentment she must have nursed for years against a destiny that prevented her from participating in the rites of Buddhism while other women of her class, and of her family, were completely free to do so; or, less melodramatically, it may be a wittily contrived subsitution for other forms of participation in worship from which she felt compelled to abstain, a means for making herself present, through a poem she crafted specifically for a special situation and event, in a place and time in which she herself could not be.

The composing of *Hosshin wakashū*, over ten years after this exchange with Higashi Sanjō-in, was perhaps also an attempt to assuage the resentments and anxieties that may have resulted from Senshi's enforced neglect of Buddhist devotions, but surely, like this Mitarashigawa poem, it was conceived as an alternative, but in no sense secondary, means of expressing sincere faith and of enacting a kind of intimate encounter and exchange with the revered vessels of that faith: the Buddhist scriptures, which were themselves objects of reverence, both physically and in the abstract. Ostensibly, Senshi should not have had much to do with them: she should not have spent much time reading or studying them, and should certainly not have had direct contact with learned monks who might otherwise have explicated them to her. But obviously, in this case as in others, the letter of the legal codes carried far less weight with her than did the awesome words of the Buddhist canon. No records or memoirs reveal precisely how Senshi gained her knowledge of Buddhist scripture. Perhaps her knowledge of it was not extraordinarily vast or deep, but about the same as the average well-educated royal or noble laywoman

---

62. In *Daisaiin saki no gyoshū* no. 282, "Muma" explicitly compares the Priestess to a long-lived tortoise. In that instance, the tortoise is a figurine involved in games accompanying a "firefly contest" (*hotaru awase*), probably a session for composing poems on summer themes.

would have had. But there was one great difference in her case: in some sense, if only technically rather than practically, her involvement with Buddhist texts, whatever form it took, was a subversion of the unique customs that supposedly governed her behavior and activities. Things may have been the other way around, of course: she may have viewed the official or customary restrictions as unreasonable, even outrageous subversions of her natural right to do as other women might do, at least in the sphere of religious study and practice. But, after all, she lived the greater part of her life—including the period during which she wrote her "Buddhist poems"—in an extraordinary sphere, and perhaps the very length of the time spent thus was what allowed her to cultivate a sense of her own way of doing things and a conviction that she had a right to do them that way.

It is tempting to imagine how often Senshi must have asked herself "Why me?"—that is, why she, of all women who might potentially have done so, had to be the one not only to serve as Saiin but to serve for such an exceptionally long time. The post of Saiin was created in 810 by Emperor Saga and was filled for the first time by his daughter, Uchiko; the motive seems to have been to flatter the Kamo deities (principally Kamo Wake Ikazuchi no mikoto in the upper shrine, Tamayorihime no mikoto and Kamo Taketsunumi no mikoto in the lower shrine[63]) by creating a post similar to that of the High Priestess of the Ise Shrines and thereby to enlist their aid in suppressing the efforts of Fujiwara Kusuko to put her husband, the ex-emperor Heizei, back on the throne. One effect, besides the crushing of Kusuko's revolt, was the forging of closer ties than had existed before between the Kamo cult and the imperial family, and so, until early in the thirteenth century, the post of Saiin was continuously filled by young female relatives of reigning emperors. Ostensibly, a new Kamo priestess was to be chosen at the beginning of each reign, by divination, from among the unmarried female kin of the new emperor. After a period of ritual purification, usually lasting some months, the new priestess underwent a final ceremony of ritual cleansing in the waters of the Kamo River and then was installed in the official residence at Murasakino, which lay about halfway between the upper and lower Kamo Shrines.[64] Her chief

---

63. The two shrines are familiarly known as Kamigamo Jinja and Shimogamo Jinja, "upper Kamo shrine" and "lower Kamo shrine," respectively. The official name of the "upper" shrine is Kamo Wake Ikazuchi Jinja, and one other name for the "lower" shrine, which lies downstream and to the southeast of the "upper," is "Kamo Mioya ['esteemed parent'] Jinja," indicating a family relationship among the Kamo deities: Tamayorihime is the mother of Wake Ikazuchi, and Taketsunumi is the father of Tamayorihime.

64. See McCullough and McCullough, *A Tale of Flowering Fortunes*, supplementary n. 25, 386–88.

task thereafter was to preside over the annual observances of the Kamo festival, around the middle of the fourth month, and to participate in a number of other lesser rituals associated with the Kamo Shrines. Shortly before each Kamo festival, the priestess repeated her lustrations in the Kamo River; on the main festival day, the entire court and much of the city assembled along Ichijō ōji, the northernmost east-west avenue of the capital, to watch the colorful procession that accompanied her to the lower Kamo Shrine, where she made offerings, and then to the upper, where the priestess passed the night. Next day, in a slightly less elaborate procession, she made her way back to the Murasakino residence, where, for the most part, she would remain until the festival of the following year— maintaining a constant vigil against all sources of pollution that might impair her capacity to serve the gods and the state.

On the third day of the fourth month of Ten'en 3 (975), the mother of Sonshi, the current Saiin, died. (This is the Sonshi mentioned above as the woman for whom *Sanbōe* was written in the following decade.) Because of her mother's death, Sonshi was unable to participate in the Kamo festival, which was scheduled a few days later, and on the eighteenth she left Murasakino for good. On the twenty-fifth day of the sixth month, the twelve-year-old Senshi, tenth daughter of the reigning emperor Murakami, was chosen as her successor. The choice was surely determined by certain factors besides the oracular: for one thing, her bloodlines were impeccable, since her mother, Fujiwara Anshi, who died just four days after giving birth to her, was a daughter of Morosuke (908–60), Minister of the Right during her father's reign, whose son, Kanemichi (925–77) was both *dajōdaijin* (chancellor) and *kanpaku* (regent) for the reigning emperor, Senshi's brother En'yū. Nor was she by any means too young for the post: a large number of the women who served as either Saiin or Saigū were named to their offices as children. Senshi had not completed all her rites of purification by the time of the next Kamo festival, but she did take up residence at Murasakino soon thereafter, in the fourth month of 977.[65] It was to be her residence until 1031, by which time she was sixty-eight years old.

There was certainly a precedent for keeping a Saiin on through a change of emperor: Sonshi, for example, had begun her service at Kamo during her father Reizei's reign and had continued even after he abdicated and was succeeded by his brother En'yū. But no one ever did what Senshi

---

65. *Kamo Saiin ki* (anonymous and undated), in Hanawa, ed., *Gunsho ruijū* 3, 6–7. For a detailed chronology of these and other events in Senshi's life, see Tokoro Kyōko, "Senshi Naishinnō nenpu kō," *Kodai bunka* 36.4 (April 1984): 28–41. In the English translation of the table of contents of this periodical, the Saiin's name is given as "Nobuko," but in later publications Tokoro adheres to the standard reading, "Senshi."

did: she went on and on, through the reigns of En'yū, Kazan (her nephew), Ichijō (another nephew), Sanjō (another nephew), and into the reign of Goichijō (her grandnephew). No doubt Senshi would have liked to retire long before she did, and it is not entirely clear why she did not do so. Perhaps she was asked to remain by those who determined such things—the men who held political power at the time were all close cousins, including her first cousin Michinaga—out of fear of the deleterious effect that a change might cause, or perhaps, as has been suggested, because there were no really good (i.e., politically neutral) candidates to replace her.[66]

The greatness that earned her the appellation *"Daisaiin"* was not only the greatness of her years (she lived much longer than most men and women did in her day) or her tenacity as High Priestess.[67] The diaries of her literary contemporaries are ample in their expressions of respect for her character, deportment, and taste, though the praise is tempered by the mild spirit of rivalry that existed between the Saiin retinue and those of the great ladies of the imperial court. The observations of Murasaki Shikibu and Sei Shōnagon, each of whom served one of her nephew Ichijō's consorts, are typically perspicacious and competitive. In a section of her diary in which she evaluates the reputations of various ladies in aristocratic service, Murasaki is extremely critical of the pretensions of a Saiin attendant, one "Chūjō," whose letter Murasaki has seen by chance:

How could she be so odious? I realize it was a personal letter, but she had actually written: 'When it comes to judging poetry, who can rival our Princess [i.e. Senshi]? She is the only one who could recognize a promising talent nowadays!' There may be some point in what she says, but if she claims that much for her circle of friends, then how is it they produce so few poems of merit? Admittedly they do seem to be very elegant and sophisticated, but were you to make a comparison, I doubt they would necessarily prove to be any better than the women I see around me. They keep very much to themselves. Whenever I have visited them, for it is a place famous for beautiful moonlit nights, marvellous dawn skies, cherries, and the song of the wood thrush, the High Priestess has always seemed most sensitive. The place has an aura of seclusion and mystery about it, and they have very little to distract them. Rarely are they ever in the rush we are whenever Her

66. Okazaki, "Daisaiin Senshi no kenkyū," 129.

67. Tokoro points out that another Kamo priestess, Emperor Daigo's daughter Onshi, was also referred to as "Daisaiin." She served through two relatively long reigns, Suzaku's and Murakami's, for some thirty-six and a half years. Tokoro, "Senshi Naishinnō nenpu kō," 41.

Majesty visits the Emperor, or His Excellency [Michinaga] decides to come and stay the night. Indeed, the place naturally lends itself to poetry. Amid such perfect elegance, how could one possibly fail to produce anything but excellent poems?[68]

So, in Murasaki's eyes, even if the products were not as impressive as they might be, the Saiin was at least potentially a very fine place in which to live quietly, devoting most of one's time to learning and practicing the art of poetry, with Senshi as mentor. Likewise, Sei Shōnagon, in *Makura no sōshi*, listed the Saiin right after the palace and the private households of imperial consorts and princesses of the first rank as desirable places in which ladies of good birth might serve their superiors. But she too saw a problem: "Though the Saiin is a terribly sinful place," she wrote, "it is charming nonetheless (*Saiin tsumifukakanaredo okashi*)."[69] The perceived or putative sinfulness, of course, did not arise from scandalous behavior but from the prohibitions that forced the denizens of the Saiin to neglect the Buddhist devotions that would have been a normal part of life in any other lady's household. At the Saiin, there was (again, at least in theory) no sutra copying to be done, there were no lectures by bright, inspiring preachers, nor even the freedom to utter the Buddha's name out loud.[70]

In *Genji monogatari*, the characters who serve either as Saigū or Saiin are extremely anxious about this neglect and the resultant "sinfulness": the princess Asagao, for example, is very eager to counteract this evil by taking vows as soon as she can once her period of service as Saiin is at an end. It is evident from both her public and private behavior that this was probably an intention nursed by Senshi for a very long time, too. Such a desire was surely what prompted her pronouncement—"*Sanagara tomo ni*

68. Richard Bowring, trans., *Murasaki Shikibu: Her Diary and Poetic Memoirs* (Princeton: Princeton University Press, 1982), 123–24. See also Ikeda Kikan and Akiyama Ken, eds., *Murasaki Shikibu nikki* (NKBT 19), 490–91.

69. Ikeda Kikan and Kishigami Shinji, eds., *Makura no sōshi* (NKBT 19), 328. See also the "*shiki no mizōshi ni owashimasu koro*" section, in which the empress Teishi gets extremely anxious about the preparation of poems to be sent in response to those received from the Saiin.

70. *Daisaiin gyoshū* (nos. 90–91) records an exchange between some Saiin women and an apparently well-known (and good looking?) preacher, Ninkō Shōnin. When "Mibu" went to hear him preach, she took a letter from some of the other women in which they said they were "dying to meet him in the Pure Land" (*monoguruhoshiu gokuraku ni matsubeki*); in a poem he sent back to them, he asked how they expected to achieve the Pure Land if all they could do was make jokes about it, and in turn they retorted, "a troth made with a saint, even in jest, should produce the seeds of Buddhahood!" The whole episode is rather reminiscent of the attitudes toward the priesthood described in *Makura no sōshi* (for example, in the *dan* beginning "*Sekkyō no kōji wa . . .* in NKBT 19, 73), and reveals an aspect of women's views of the clergy and what it represented that is very different from the pious sentiments emphasized here.

hotoke to naramu"—in the midst of the Kamo festivities, as reported in
Ōkagami, which also observes (in the present tense, since she would have
been alive at the time that the *Ōkagami* narration is supposed to take
place), that "concerned though the Princess may be with the life to come,
she does not disregard worldly splendor," and continues with anecdotes
about her gracious—and politically astute—dealings with the brash, all-
powerful Michinaga.[71] The woman whom the world saw in the Kamo
procession was cool and reserved but secure enough in the prestige of her
position to risk an open display of religious sentiments not wholly in
keeping with that setting. There seems to have been no censure of her
declaration (the *Ōkagami* narrator does observe that she may have gone "a
little too far"[72]) but, if anything, an increase in public admiration for her
poise and her determination, like that of a bodhisattva, to share her conviction with others.

Back at the Murasakino mansion, however, she was alone with her
budding poets and the responsibilities that distracted her, even if they did
not wholly prevent her, from pursuing her own way toward Buddhist
salvation. Like her companions, she could not stop her ears against the
sounds that came from those in the outside world who were able to
pursue that goal more freely than she was. According to the *kotobagaki* to a
poem (no. 671) in the second "miscellaneous" section of *Kin'yō wakashū*,
she awoke one moonlit night in the eighth month to the sound of the
chanting of a passing "*Amida hijiri*"—an itinerant monk devoted to worshiping Amida Buddha by intoning his name. Rather boldly, she had the
monk brought into the house and had him deliver these lines to an
attendant at home on leave of absence (*Hachigatsu bakari ni tsuki akakarikeru
yo Amida no hijiri no tōrikeru o yobiyosesasete sato naru nyōbō ni iitsu-
kawashikeru*):

> *Amidabu to tonauru koe ni yume samete
> nishi e katabuku tsuki o koso mire*[73]

---

71. McCullough, *Ōkagami*, 133; see also *NKBT* 21, 123–24. In one of these anecdotes,
Senshi and Michinaga exchange flattering poems after a Kamo festival procession
during which Senshi was shown her imperial grandnephews in the arms of their
proud maternal grandfather, Michinaga. The poems both make use of the double
meaning of the word *auhi*, "day of meeting" (in reference to the familial encounter)
and "heartvine" (one of the floral emblems of the festival). These poems also appear in
Goshūi wakashū (nos. 1107 and 1108) in *SKT* 1, 137.
   The *Ōkagami* narration is supposed to take place at the Urin'in, close to the Saiin's
residence, and the narrator claims that Senshi is a regular patroness of the annual rite,
the *Bodaikō* ("Enlightenment Service"), which is the occasion for his telling of his tale.

72. McCullough, *Ōkagami*, 133.

73. Ishihara, *Shakkyōka no kenkyū*, 98. A slightly different version is in *SKT* 1, 155.

Awakened from my dreams by a voice that chanted "Amida
   Buddha,"
   it was the moon setting in the west that I saw.

The voice that broke the stillness of the night brought Senshi out of her
dreams (*yume*)—and her use of this word, which also stands for the
confused state of the unenlightened person, also suggests that hearing
Amida's name pierce the darkness has brought new clarity to her mind. It
has, at any rate, allowed her to see his symbol, the moon once again,
declining over the western horizon toward his Pure Land (as it did when
Muma yearned after it as she listened to the carriages returning from the
Urin'in to court)—and perhaps also in the direction to which this message
to her absent companion was to be sent. Barriers of one kind or another
might lie between Senshi and the path she sought, but, this poem seems
to suggest, signs and sounds of faith and of the faithful could not fail to
reach her and to have their impact upon her as upon all others.

   Pure Land proselytizers like this *Amida hijiri* and others did have a
considerable impact on the aristocracy, whose demonstrations and expressions of their yearning for rebirth in Amida's paradise became more
and more conspicuous toward the end of the tenth century. This seems to
have been particularly so in the decade of the 980s, when, for both personal and political reasons, a number of Senshi's own close relatives took
the greatest step toward their salvation that they could take: *shukke*. Her
half brother Prince Munehira took vows in 981. Her niece Sonshi, who
had become one of Emperor En'yū's wives, did so in 982, probably because of illness. Her brother En'yū, having retired from the throne, took
vows in 985. Her nephew Kazan, Sonshi's brother, followed suit when he
was forced to abdicate in 986. Her elder sister Shishi had already done so
at the beginning of that year, a few months before her death.[74] But Senshi
remained just as she was, growing older while the years of her Kamo
service went on and on. She was sixty-three in the first month of 1026
when the news reached her that the dowager empress Jōtōmon'in (her
cousin Michinaga's daughter, wife of her nephew Emperor Ichijō and
mother of two emperors, Senshi's grandnephews Goichijō and Gosuzaku)
had taken her vows. The poem Senshi sent her appears in the "miscellaneous" section of *Goshūi wakashū* (no. 1027[75]) and in *Eiga monogatari* as
well[76]:

---

74. Sasaki, "Daisaiin Senshi Naishinnō no waka," 243–44.

75. *SKT* 1, 134.

76. *NKBT* 76, 265; McCullough and McCullough, *A Tale of Flowering Fortunes*, 715.

kimi sura mo makoto no michi ni irinunari
hitori ya nagaki yami ni madowamu
I hear that now you, too, have entered upon the true way;
shall I alone remain lost in the endless darkness?

Here, as in many poems in *Hosshin wakashū*, Senshi used the darkness that envelops the path of the unenlightened—the same dark path of Izumi Shikibu's famous poem—as an emblem for her own state, contrasting it with the brilliantly lit path of those who have found the true way (*makoto no michi*) to take through their lives. As long as she continued as Saiin, her life remained enshrouded in that same darkness, lost in those same dreams. In the late years of her career, as it is described in *Konjaku monogatari shū* (no doubt with some exaggeration) the brilliance of the Saiin establishment was also dimmed: chance visitors were shocked by the dilapidated condition of the Murasakino mansion but were nevertheless charmed by the air of antique refinement that filled the shadowy gardens that had been so resplendent in Murasaki Shikibu's day; meanwhile, the aging Senshi still prayed faithfully and constantly to Amida.[77] In the fullness of her years, this trespass against the Kamo customs was beyond reproach—in spite of what Norinaga and others might have to say about it later on.

Finally, in the ninth month of Chōgen 4 (1031), claiming infirmity, Senshi asked to be relieved of her post. Before official sanction for her retirement had been granted, she left the Murasakino mansion for her private residence, the Muromachi palace. Six days later she took her first vows as a Buddhist nun from the monk Jinkaku, her maternal uncle; a few weeks later, the learned Tendai monk Kakuchō conducted the rite called *jikkai* for her, whereby she swore to uphold the ten fundamental precepts of a novice nun. She was too ill to make the trip to Karasaki, on the shores of Lake Biwa, where a rite of release for retiring Kamo priestesses was usually conducted. But it was four more years before she died, at the Muromachi palace, in the sixth month of Chōgen 8 (1035), having reached the age of 72.[78]

---

77. See *Konjaku monogatari shū* 19.17 in Yamada Yoshio, Yamada Tadao, Yamada Hideo, and Yamada Toshio, eds., *Konjaku monogatari shū* 4 (*NKBT* 25), 97–99.

78. *Sakeiki*, the diary of Minamoto Tsuneyori, then *Saiin bettō* (the court-appointed superintendent of the Saiin office) provides the most detailed account of Senshi's retirement. See *Sakeiki*, in *Zōho shiryō taisei* Kankōkai, ed., *Zōho shiryō taisei* 6 (Kyoto: Rinsen Shoten, 1965), 293–301; the relevant passages are quoted in Okazaki, "Daisaiin Senshi no kenkyū," 124–25. See also Tokoro, "Senshi Naishinnō nenpu kō," 36–37. *Konjaku monogatari shū* 19.17 incorrectly names the priest Keiso (or Kyōso) of Miidera (Onjōji) as Senshi's preceptor. He died in 1019, twelve years before the recorded date of Senshi's retirement.

Some forty-three years earlier, when she wrote *Hosshin wakashū*, she was full of both frustration and hope. (In the fourth month of 1012, four months before she completed the cycle, she had been informed, for neither the first nor last time, that there would be no change of Saiin despite the fact that a new emperor had come to the throne.[79]) Though unable to pursue the kind of religious life that she may have liked to have had, she was free, in the privacy of her home, to bring the words of Buddhist scripture into the serious games of poem making that filled the days and nights she shared with her women companions. She perceived, as the *Hosshin wakashū* preface explains it, that since other forms of devotion were inappropriate—she could not commission the construction of "halls and pagodas," as the great men of her family could, or "shave her head" and live the life of an ascetic on some mountainside, as others might—the writing of such a work was by far the best thing that she could do, as well as the most apt way for her to employ her literary expertise.

Her commitment to and love of literature—the strongest element of her bond with the women who dwelt with her at Murasakino—is probably what really lies behind the old and probably apocryphal story about the role she may have had in bringing about the writing of *Genji monogatari*: she supposedly asked the empress Shōshi (the latter-day Jōtōmon'in) if her women had any new romances to share with the women of the Saiin, whereupon Murasaki Shikibu undertook to produce one.[80] We may think

---

79. Tokoro, "Senshi Naishinnō nenpu kō," 33.

80. There are no contemporary records of this exchange; the earliest account of it appears in Yotsutsuji Yoshinari's commentary on *Genji*, the *Kakaishō*, completed in 1367. See Muromatsu Iwao, ed., *Kokubun chūshaku zensho* 3 (Tokyo: Kokugakuin Daigaku Shuppanbu, 1908), 1. On the other hand, there is evidence of other kinds of personal exchanges between the two women. Michinaga's diary, known as *Midō kanpaku ki*, notes that on the day of the Kamo festival in the fourth month of Kankō 1 (1004), the empress sent the priestess a fan; in the seventh month of Kankō 6 (1009), the priestess sent the empress a *biwa* (Japanese lute) and a *kin* (a seven-stringed *koto*). See Tōkyō Daigaku Shiryō Hensan Sho, ed., *Midō kanpaku ki* (*Dai Nihon Kokiroku*) (Tokyo: Iwanami Shoten, 1952–54), vol. 1, 85, and vol. 2, 9.

Also, according to the *kotobagaki* for poem 1109 in *Goshūi wakashū*, Senshi sent the following to the empress the day after a Kamo festival during which Shōshi, accompanying the emperor, attended part of the ceremonies but returned to the palace without stopping at Murasakino to visit in person with the priestess:

> *miyuki seshi kamo no kawanami kaerusa ni*
> *tachi ya yoru to zo machiakashitsuru*
> In the wake of your royal visit to the Kamo River waters,
>   I lay awake 'til dawn in hope that you might stop here.

(*SKT* 1, 137). *Kamo no kawanami* is "waves in the Kamo River" but also attaches to *miyuki seshi kamo* to suggest, "Did you really come here, or not?"—a frequent posture in poems about visits (usually between lovers) that do not come to pass, or end so quickly that they seem never to have occurred. *Tats[u]* and *yor[u]*, here combined to mean "stop by and pay a visit," are also verbs associated with the action of waves. This intricate poem pays ample respect to the empress but may also express real regret over the two women's failure or inability to take advantage of an opportunity to meet face to face.

of *Hosshin wakashū* as yet another literary work that was meant, first of all, to be shared by Senshi with the Saiin women, and indeed, many of its passages from scripture and the poems on them focus closely on images and messages of particular significance for women. The famous Murasakino moonlight that Murasaki Shikibu recalled so vividly is there, too, but it is transformed into the light of a moon that represents the fulfilled promise of salvation—a promise not given to or taken by these women without restrictions, but a promise that they wanted very much to believe in. *Hosshin wakashū* itself was written to help them toward its realization—and to show them what might be done when the art of *waka* was enlisted in that endeavor.

PART TWO
A READING OF *HOSSHIN WAKASHŪ*

No original or early text of *Hosshin wakashū* survives, and the earliest evidence for its existence and its authorship is in those anthologies that include poems selected from it. Even at that, the earliest *chokusenshū* to include a *Hosshin wakashū* poem is the *Shin kokin wakashū*, the compilation of which was completed in 1205.[1] The three bona fide manuscript copies of *Hosshin wakashū* that exist today are all undated but very late—probably "early *kinsei*" (i.e., seventeenth century), according to Ishihara Kiyoshi—and all are very similar to one another in most respects. Two are held by the Shoryōbu, the library of the Imperial Household Ministry (Kunaichō) on the grounds of the Imperial Palace in Tokyo, and the other is in the Matsudaira collection in the City of Shimabara Community Hall (Shimabara Shiritsu Kōminkan) in Nagasaki Prefecture. (Hereafter these copies shall be referred to as "Shoryōbu A," "Shoryōbu B," and "the Matsudaira Bunko copy."[2])

---

1. *Shin kokin wakashū* no. 1971, the *kotobagaki* of which identifies it as "a poem from *Hosshin wakashū*," is HSWKS no. 49. Fujiwara Teika, one of the *Shin kokin wakashū* editors, also included a three-poem sequence, consisting of HSWKS poems 5, 12, and 47, as poems 588–90 in *Shin chokusen wakashū*, which he compiled in 1234–35. The other *chokusenshū* that include HSWKS poems are:

    Shoku gosen wakashū, compiled in 1251; nos. 589, 616, and 617 are HSWKS nos. 45, 21, and 14;
    Shoku shūi wakashū, compiled in 1278; nos. 1344 and 1348 are HSWKS nos. 15 and 28;
    Gyokuyō wakashū, compiled in 1312; no. 2619 is HSWKS no. 33;
    Shoku senzai wakashū, compiled in 1320; no. 384 is also HSWKS no. 33;
    and *Shoku goshūi wakashū*, compiled in 1325; nos. 1271 and 1278 are HSWKS nos. 24 and 34.

    See also Ishihara, *Hosshin wakashū no kenkyū* (Osaka: Izumi Shoin, 1983), 260–67 for a compilation of all of Senshi's poems that are included in *chokusenshū*.

2. All three are hand-calligraphed folded-paper books with hand-sewn bindings. One of the two Shoryōbu copies (designated the *kōbon*, our "Shoryōbu A," by Ishihara) is of the type called *masugata retchōsō* (or *yamato toji*), a small, square book of folded pages, with poems recorded on both folded sides, bound with a cover by a small cord that passes through holes made close to the unfolded edge. The other Shoryōbu copy (Ishihara's *itsubon*, our "Shoryōbu B") and the Matsudaira Bunko copy are both of the type called *fukuro toji*, with oblong folded pages stitched together at the unfolded edges. These are formats commonly used for copies of poetry collections. There is no colophon (*okugaki*) in Shoryōbu A, but the colophon in Shoryōbu B says that it was made from another copy executed in 1245 (Kangen 3) by "Tō [Fuji] Dainagon," identified as Fujiwara Tameie (1198–1275), son of Teika and a distinguished courtier, poet, and editor of anthologies. Ishihara observes that the calligraphic style of this Shoryōbu copy resembles that of Emperor Reigen (1654–1732, reigned 1663–87), and that the relationship between this copy and the Matsudaira Bunko copy is particularly close (Ishihara, *Hosshin wakashū no kenkyū*, 66).

These three copies are the basis of all modern editions of *Hosshin wakashū*. Of the three, only the Matsudaira Bunko copy is available in photo-reprinted format, in Ishihara's *Hosshin wakashū no kenkyū* (1983). Serious lacunae occur in only a handful of the fifty-five poems, and orthographic discrepancies among the three copies are, with a few exceptions, minor. These are most satisfactorily resolved in Hashimoto Yuri's edition of the cycle in the *shikashū* volume of *Shinpen kokka taikan*.[3]

In all three copies, the topic-lines, in Chinese, are written in a very clear, regulated style, while the *waka* are copied in a much more cursive hand. Thus, the two types of text within the text are clearly demarcated. Generally, the *waka* texts occupy the full height of the page; in Shoryōbu A, the smallest book of the three, the *waka* had to be written in more than one column, but, as is customary, there is no regular point (in terms of meter or any other formal characteristic) at which the break is made. In all of the copies, the text of the preface also occupies the full height of the page, while the topic-quotation texts are indented (though not consistently in the Shoryōbu texts), with a further indentation where the title of the source of the quotation is given. There is no way of knowing whether this was the format of the holograph, but in these copies the divisions between and relationships among the various parts of the text are very easily recognized.

Although there is no holograph, no one questions the authenticity of *Hosshin wakashū* and no one suggests that it was written by anyone other than Senshi. In this case, the latter-day *chokusenshū* editors' attributions are considered reliable. Still, it is frustrating not to have an earlier, if not a contemporary or near-contemporary, attribution; instead, we have to settle for one that is accepted largely by convention. The association of an easily identifiable persona with a text is yet another of the things that gives it context, and provides its readers with a comfortable and satisfyingly nostalgic way of reading it—a way of reading that is accompanied by an imagining of a moment in the past when that persona wrote that text, a moment filled with all the factors that, one may suppose, moved her to write it as she did. Traditionally, *Hosshin wakashū* is read with Senshi very much in mind, despite the fact that absolute proof of her authorship is missing. A reading of the same text without her would be less sentimental, but drier and duller, and most readers have chosen to keep her there.

The most thorough modern reading of *Hosshin wakashū* is Ishihara Kiyoshi's, and it is a reading to which a strong image of a pious and

---

3. *SKT* 3, 292–94, reproduced herein in the appendix; see also Hashimoto's explanatory notes on p. 890 of the same volume.

insightful Senshi—the Senshi of *setsuwa, rekishi-monogatari,* and the *"omoedomo"* poem as traditionally read—is central. Ishihara sees each *waka* in the work as an intense adoration of the scriptural text on which it is based, and he repeatedly points to Senshi's sophisticated comprehension of those scriptural texts, as revealed in the *waka.* That the poet was capable of such achievements can reasonably be posited on the basis of a reading of the text that presupposes a Senshi with fervent religious aspirations and extensive training in scriptural interpretation. These may be reasonable presuppositions, though largely undocumented except by the poems themselves (which makes the reasoning circular) and by the general example of aristocratic women of her time as we perceive them, again, largely on the basis of their works and, secondarily, through accounts by their contemporaries. But if the text itself is kept in the foreground, it need not be supplanted by an overly potent and overly romanticized image of its author—and it will reveal things that the interference of this image may inadvertently mask.

Ishihara's reading of each poem as an intense response to each passage on which it is based rightly emphasizes the close relationship between the two parts of each *dai-and-tanka* pair. But his approach creates several problems. It obscures the relationship of each *dai-and-tanka* pair to all the others and disrupts the reader's sense of the integrity of the work as a sustained devotional/literary exercise and as a cycle. *Hosshin wakashū* is cyclical in the sense that certain topics and themes recur within it, rising to the surface in response to promptings from the topic-texts, which may themselves be cyclically orchestrated. In both quotations and poems, for example, darkness and light, and their imagery, succeed one another repeatedly (see, for instance, the sequence 33–35), reflecting and often accompanying the poem-speaker's thematic shifts between doubts about her capacity to attain salvation—especially in response to texts that decree that she, as a woman, faces special obstacles in her path to Buddhahood[4]—and the displacement of those doubts by confident acceptance of the promise of salvation for all. The cyclical shape of the whole is generated in great part by the relationships among the topic-texts, which offer sets of motifs, topoi, and language structures that, for various reasons, captured the interest of the selector at the outset. Achievement of a certain kind of thematic or cyclical unity among them may have been one objective, but another and perhaps paramount factor must have been the desire to make appropriate selections, useful for poem making, from a representative assortment of scriptural sources.

---

4. For further discussion of these "obstacles," see n. 16, below.

In his commentary on each poem, Ishihara includes a much more broadly cut swatch of the original scriptural text that contains the topic-quotation than that reproduced in *Hosshin wakashū* itself. He then analyzes each poem as one that fully encompasses the broader implications of the larger passage, or of the whole work that, in his view, it represents. But in many cases, a consideration of the topic-quotations and accompanying poems as they stand in the text suggests, rather, that the poet's attention was fixed primarily on the quotations as isolated passages and on the elements therein that could best serve her in the process of making new poems. The poems in sequences 41–42–43 and 44–45–46 are excellent illustrations of this process. The topic-texts and the discrete elements the poet selects from them to work into the poems are not necessarily of great doctrinal significance, nor particularly germane to the purport of the chapters of the *Lotus* that are their source, and they are quite roughly cut from the original context. This suggests that the selector sought them out particularly for those useful, discrete elements that they happen to contain. The poems yielded by this selective process do not encompass or represent in condensation the full purport of whole chapters any more than the isolated quotations can be said to do. Ishihara's keen interest in Senshi as a pious and knowledgeable reader thus causes him to ignore her as a working craftswoman, piecing her text together with discretion, mustering all her *waka* expertise and ingenuity to a challenging but potentially rewarding task.

Ishihara almost always takes the voice or voices of the topic-text—as broadly conceived—to be identical with the voice or voices in the *waka*, and in some cases he does so where other possibilities—at least, the possibility of ambiguity, intentional or otherwise—clearly exist. A sensitivity to the cyclical character of *Hosshin wakashū* as a whole carries with it a sensitivity to the poet's manipulation of voice, or rather voices, which at some points does replicate the position and "speech" of personae in the quoted passages but, at the same time, implies the functioning of another identity who may appropriate, alter, and sometimes even invert the meaning of the original "speaker." (In poem 22, the poem-speaker's reference to her "own name," *wagana,* marks the entry into the discourse of an identity quite distinct from that which speaks in the preceding quotation, and it is an identity who doubly inverts the significance of the words "my name" in the quotation. In poems 9, 20, and 29, *wagami,* "my self," marks a similar assertion of the poem-speaker's self-naming identity.) The way that each poem responds to the text on which it is based is not the same throughout the work: it is, rather, a constantly shifting relationship, and the shifts must have as much to do with the ways that the author read the topic-texts as they do with the different means for poem making with which she was supplied by each topic-text and her perception of the problems and possibilties that it presented.

In discussing these relationships Ishihara is chiefly concerned with overt content and underlying theme; for the most part, he does not examine what is most immediate, the specific ways in which the elements of each *dai*-and-*waka* pair—words, images, metaphors—correspond or do not correspond, or are transposed or transformed. Nor does Ishihara pay adequate attention to the elements that have been interpolated in order to make the poems poems. Thus, his emphasis on the pietistic character of the work drastically (and ironically) de-emphasizes its poetic and literary character. Ishihara's treatment of the poems in *Hosshin wakashū* is essentially the same as his treatment of *Shakkyōka* in general, and it is firmly grounded in his concept of that genre.[5] But, again, if the genre concept is not allowed to steal the foreground from the text itself, the text can then present itself as whatever it may be. Clearly, it was written out of devotion, with sincere religious motivation, but also out of devotion to the art of poetry itself, without any preconception and through no process that would create any rupture between it and the traditions and canons of secular poetry. The poems of *Hosshin wakashū* can and should be read as poems that are functionally and structurally very similar to other Japanese poems of their time, just as are most other poems that, sooner or later, received generic labeling as *Shakkyōka*.

The *Hosshin wakashū* preface itself makes this clear with its argument that the poems that follow are not only akin to the Buddha's own hymns of praise but are also concurrent with the very mainstream of the Japanese poetic tradition. The preface invites its readers to read this as Senshi's argument, and no critic has seriously suggested that the preface is the work of anyone but her. It certainly "speaks" in her voice. It is, however, rare to find a *waka* collection introduced by a preface in Chinese, whether the collection is comprised of works by a man or by a woman.[6] In this preface, as part of her justification of the choice of *waka* as her medium, the author suggests that she would not be very comfortable writing in any language but Japanese. One may suppose, therefore (although it cannot be proven), that Senshi had someone write the preface for her, that she

---

5. See Ishihara, *Shakkyōka no kenkyū*, 11–24.

6. The *manajo* of the *Kokin wakashū* may be set aside as a special case, as may the other prefaces in Chinese modeled on it for later *chokusenshū*—collections that are far more organized and formal than the *shikashū* are. Ōe Chisato's *Kudai waka* is one *shikashū* that does have a short preface in Chinese. Of the 159 collections included in the *shikashū* volumes of *SKT*, only a very few have any sort of preface at all. Of those by women that predate Senshi's collections, none has a preface in Chinese and only one, *Kamo no Yasunori nyo shū*, has any preface at all; it is a very long one, in *kana*. See *SKT* 3, 146, 198–201.

dictated its purport and general content to a scribe (perhaps, but not necessarily, male) who then expressed her ideas in a fairly standard Sino-Japanese rhetorical style. Some specific correspondences between elements of its rhetoric and that of *waka* treatises written much later (as shall be noted below) may give rise to suspicions that this preface is a "forgery" of the Kamakura or even a later era.[7] Still, it is also possible that Senshi herself composed it and that later "theorists" wrote as they did in direct or indirect imitation of her. And perhaps the fact that it is written in Chinese does not pose as great a problem as it seems. Much of the rest of *Hosshin wakashū*— the portion culled from scripture—is inscribed in that language too, so perhaps this "Chinese" preface was written thus so as to share in the scripture's authority by association, while proffering a high-minded rationale for the accompanying exercise in *waka*—a language and tradition with a different but not necessarily lesser authority of its own. Furthermore, Senshi's treatment of the quotations used as *dai* for the *Hosshin wakashū* poems does suggest that she read Chinese well, so perhaps she (like her forerunner Uchiko, skilled in both Chinese and Japanese) had been trained to write it, too, no matter what the preface says. The following is a translation of what it does say:

[PREFACE]

It is in the hope of attaining enlightenment that I have for some time been directing all my thoughts to the Buddha and devoting my heart to his teachings. When Śākyamuni Buddha propounded the Single Vehicle in the *Lotus Sutra*, he sang the praises of all the Tathāgatas in verse: thus do we know that the composition of verses is very meritorious and that it is a form of Buddhist worship. Now Sanskrit is an Indian language, and India lies far across the desert sands; *kanji* are a Chinese invention, and the customs of China are very different from ours. I was born in Japan, and received the body of a woman: I cannot imitate the manners of those foreign places, and my sensibilities are wholly those of my homeland. I have studied the thirty-one syllable poetry invented by Susa-no-o, and have nurtured this tradition; and when I practice in the

---

7. I am indebted to Robert N. Huey for pointing out the correspondences between the *HSWKS* preface and specific works of later times, which shall be discussed below.

style of the thirty-one character verse offered by the starving man of Kataoka, his words are my models. Here, I
begin with poems on the Four Vast Vows and go on to
poems on the Ten Great Vows. There are, in all, fifty-five
poems brought together in this one scroll, which I call
Hosshin wakashū ("A Collection of Japanese Poems for the
Awakening of Faith"). This is because they are designed to
establish the conditions whereby all who read them will,
when given the opportunity to enter one of the Pure
Lands of the Ten Directions, be inspired with the desire to
reach Amida's paradise and ultimately be reborn there on
one of the Nine Lotus Thrones. Must I devote my re-
sources to the construction of halls and pagodas? I rely on
the truth of our Great Master's vows. Must I shave my
head and dwell in mountain forests? Better to spend my
days discovering the benefits of singing in praise. I need
not abandon the way of Japanese poetry to enter into the
practice of meditation. My only prayer is for those who
may see or hear this, in every life and every world, to join
me in admiring Prabhūtaratna's vow; and if there be anyone who condemns what I have done, let a spiritual bond
arise between them and me, wherever they may be, so
that I may treat them with respect as Sadāparibhūta
would. So devoted am I to the Three Jewels that I would
give up everything for their sake. Now I hear the autumn
wind in the trees: it warns me of the sufferings of old age.
The evening sun droops over the shadowed mountains:
does it not show me that this life, too, must come to an
end? Weeping, I ponder its bright rays. It is in the eighth
month of the ninth year of the Kankō era [1012] that I
write this.

The preface begins with a defense of poetry as a legitimate expression
of Buddhist devotion, and Śākyamuni Buddha himself, as utterer of the
Lotus Sutra, with its hymns of praise for countless Buddhas (and for itself),
is cited as one of its exemplary practitioners. But (so goes the argument)
the poetry composed in the present instance cannot be in Sanskrit, the
Buddha's language, or in Chinese, the language through which his teachings were brought to Japan, but has to be in Japanese—the poems have to
be waka—because Japanese is the only language and Japanese poetry the
only art in which the writer is truly at home. (Almost ironically, this idea

is conveyed through rather erudite Chinese rhetoric.[8]) Indeed, the writer claims, she has long schooled herself in its traditions and is fully cognizant of the debt she owes to her literary forebears. Her inheritance from them is represented by the works of two epitomes of the *waka* tradition: one is a deity, Susa-no-o no mikoto, whose *"yagumo tatsu . . ."* song is supposedly the earliest example of the thirty-one syllable *tanka* scheme, and the other is the starving beggar who, according to a very old story, exchanged verses with Prince Shōtoku when the two encountered one another at a place called Kataokayama. Susa-no-o's poem is cited by Ki no Tsurayuki in the *kana* preface to the *Kokin wakashū* as an example of Japanese poetry at the time of its origins in the "age of the gods," and this may well have been the context of Senshi's familiarity with it; the beggar's poem, though later treated as a *Shakkyōka* (because of the religious persona of its addressee rather than on the basis of content), was probably known to her through its invariable inclusion in tales about the pious and saintly prince, if not from its inclusion in *Shūi wakashū*.[9] But it is as archaic vestiges of the tradition of Japanese poetry as a whole—an essentially secular rather than religious tradition, even though these poems may in fact represent vestiges of the ritual role of early *waka*—that Senshi refers to these works: the former certainly has no Buddhist connotations, and the latter, while perhaps made more relevant to the context of *Hosshin wakashū* because of its association with the most important and legendary figure in the early history of Buddhism in Japan, is bracketed with the native deity's poem by the preface's parallel syntax and thus appears to be its equal as a representative of the indigenous lyric tradition within which Senshi places herself. The bracketing may also suggest that if that tradition could embrace the poems of a god (albeit a troublesome one) and a beggar (who

---

8. Senshi's inability to "imitate the manners of these foreign places" (India and China) is conveyed by the expressions "I cannot learn 'the *Han-tan* walk,'" a reference to a story in *Zhuang-zhi* (*Qiu-shui*) in which a youth makes a fool of himself through his clumsy mimicry of foreign customs. Similarly, in "my sensibilities are wholly those of my homeland," the word for "my homeland" is *sōshi*, i.e., *sang-zi*, a term used for "native place" at least as early as the *Hou Han shu*.

9. According to the *Kojiki*, the *"yagumo tatsu . . ."* song was sung by Susa-no-o when he took a wife and built a home in Izumo (Kurano Kenji, ed., *NKBT* 1, 89). *Nihon shoki* has the earliest version of the Kataokayama encounter and the poems it produced; later versions occur in the traditional biographies of Shōtoku Taishi (i.e., *Shōtoku Taishi denryaku, Jōgū Shōtoku Hōōtei setsu*, and *Jōgū Taishi den hoketsuki*) and in *Nihon ryōiki* (Endō Yoshimoto and Kasuga Kazuo, ed., *NKBT* 70, 77–81; see also *Sanbōe* 2.1). The prince's and the beggar's poems appear as nos. 1350 and 1351 in *Shūi wakashū*, where they are the last poems in the "Laments" chapter (*Aishō*). Ishihara treats them as part of a *Shakkyōka* group (see Ishihara, *Shakkyōka no kenkyū*, 30, 40–43), but Senshi's reference to the poem certainly does not reflect this latter-day genre classification.

may or may not have been a divine being in disguise), it could also include the works of a mortal woman.

If Senshi was really the author of this preface, as we are inclined to assume, then she was apparently the first writer to pair these two poets and their poems in a schematic account of *waka* history—but she was certainly not the last to do so. Minamoto Toshiyori (or Shunrai, 1055–1129) did so, for example, in one section of his vast *waka* treatise, known as *Toshiyori zuinō*.[10] Fujiwara Kiyosuke (1104–77) mentions the god's poem and quotes the beggar's within a few lines of *Ōgishō*,[11] and Fujiwara Shunzei (1114–1204) discusses both at some length in near succession in the historical section of *Korai fūteishō*.[12] These writers make no direct reference to *Hosshin wakashū*, so we have no evidence of their familiarity with it, and rather than posit direct lines of influence it seems best to suggest that all these writers—Senshi, or whoever wrote her preface, included—drew on a common body of evolving *waka* lore and rhetorical convention that made these poems likely candidates for service in their various arguments.[13]

In any case, Senshi's invocation of these two poets as her literary forebears must be seen as a way of associating her present work with theirs—an association that probably would not have been qualified in any way by distinctions between "secular" and "religious" poetry, distinctions that she would surely not have applied to the poems that follow this preface. Her point was exactly the opposite. Senshi certainly did not think of the poems she was writing as "*Shakkyōka*"—that is, as poems classifiable under that generic label—but as *waka*, as poetry with perhaps a special genesis and purpose, but poetry that was not so very different, after all, from the kinds of poems that she and her companions wrote when the *dai* of the moment had nothing whatsoever to do with Buddhism. She asked for no special transformation of the effect or essence of her art, as did the

---

10. According to Hashimoto Fumio, the treatise was probably written no earlier than 1111 and no later than 1114. For the passage with the two poems, see Hashimoto Fumio, Ariyoshi Tamotsu, and Fujihira Haruo, eds., *Karonshū* (*Nihon koten bungaku zenshū* 50) (Tokyo: Shōgakukan, 1975), 43–44.

11. See Sasaki Nobutsuna, ed., *Nihon kagaku taikei* 1 (Tokyo: Kazama Shobō, 1958), 222. The context is proof of the notion that *waka* is an art practiced by superhumans (since the beggar was Mañjuśrī in disguise) as well as mortals. The *Ōgishō* compilation probably took place between 1135 and 1144.

12. Hashimoto et al., eds., *Karonshū*, 278–79, 281–82.

13. There are other examples. In a treatise known as *Iwami no jo shiki* ("*Waka* rules, by a lady of the province of Iwami"; also called *Iwami no jo zuinō*), perhaps a late Heian work but more probably early Kamakura, the Kataokayama beggar's poem is highlighted in a discussion of the "four standard faults" (*shibyō*) to be avoided in *waka* composition. See Sasaki Nobutsuna, ed., *Nihon kagaku taikei* 1, 31.

men of the Kangakue when they invoked Bai Juyi's *kyōgen kigo* prayer; instead, she offered her poems just as they were, with the hope that they might take their own special place among all the others that she and her companions wrote at Murasakino, and in the belief that poems so conceived, written, and read might also aid them in their progress toward salvation.

It is to this specific end, the writer suggests, that she composed a set of fifty-five poems—beginning with four on the topic of the "Four Vast Vows" (*Shiguzeigan*) and the "Ten Great Vows" (*Jūdaigan*), both of which are statements of the goals and ideals of bodhisattvas—which are to be read as one collective work entitled *Hosshin wakashū*.[14] This name has been chosen, it is explained, because the poems' collective bodhisattva-like purpose is to help those who read them to achieve rebirth in Amida's Pure Land.

The title *Hosshin wakashū* can be understood in several ways, none of which is wholly at variance with the way that the preface presents the work it so names. The term *hosshin* is an abbreviation of *hotsu bodaishin* and is sometimes treated as a synonym for the term *anokutara sanmyaku sanbodaishin* (Sanskrit *anuttara-samyak-sambodhicitta*), "perfect enlightenment"—but in the Tendai Buddhist tradition it usually refers to the conception (*hotsu*) and the wholehearted acceptance of the desire to attain Buddhahood (*Bodaishin*), often expressed as a vow on the basis of which the nurturing of that state of mind can begin and the actions leading to that goal can be efficaciously undertaken. The cultivation and achievement of *hotsu bodaishin* is therefore a requisite early stage through which a bodhisattva (*bosatsu*) must pass in his or her progress toward Buddhahood.

Hosshin wakashū is thus an appropriate name for a collection of poems (*wakashū*) written out of the poet's bodhisattva-like desire to cultivate

---

14. The Four Vast Vows (*Shiguzeigan*) comprise a statement of the goals shared by all bodhisattvas. There is some variation in the formal and orthographical exposition of the set in texts produced or favored by different Buddhist schools. The form that Senshi uses is that found in most texts of the Tendai school; see Mochizuki Shinkō, *Bukkyō daijiten* 2, rev. ed. (Tokyo: Sekai Seiten Kankō Kyōkai, 1958–63), 1756. The Ten Great Vows (*Jūdaigan*) are associated with the bodhisattva Samantabhadra (*Fugen bosatsu*). They originally appeared in a Sanskrit verse-text entitled *Bhadracarīpranidhana*, of which there are three Chinese translations: *Monjushiri hotsugangyō* (*T* no. 296, where they are presented as vows of the bodhisattva Mañjuśrī); *Fugen bosatsu gyōgansan* (*T* no. 297); and in the last section of Prajña's forty-fascicle version of the *Kegongyō* (*T* no. 293), which is Senshi's source for poems 6–15. See *T* 10, pp. 844–48. For a brief textual history of the vows, with an English translation and a reconstructed Sanskrit text, see H. Idumi (Izumi Hōkei), "The Hymn on the Life and Vows of Samantabhadra," *The Eastern Buddhist* 5.2–3 (April 1930): 226–47. The professed object of the vows is rebirth in Amida's Pure Land, which is also established, in this preface, as Senshi's own goal and that of the composition of *HSWKS*.

hosshin in herself and in others and in the belief that both the reading and the writing of it would have that effect. It also makes sense for such a collection to begin with poems that take the *Shiguzeigan* and *Jūdaigan* as their topics, if these are indeed understood as primary statements of bodhisattva goals and bodhisattva conduct, for it is from such avowals of high purpose that the further cultivation of bodhisattvahood should proceed.[15] Yet the poet, in both the preface to her poems and in the poems themselves, shows that her desire for Buddhahood and for the enlightenment of others is already intense; in other words, it appears that the poet has already conceived of and grasped *hosshin*, in which case the poems may be read as expressions that proceed from that state rather than from a desire to bring it about or, perhaps, from a desire to cultivate the state she has already achieved while attempting to bring it out and nurture it in others.

This interpretation of the title suggests that its first element in some way qualifies or describes the second: the *waka* collected here are what might be called "*hosshin waka*" (if the term existed), that is, Japanese poems that somehow may induce or inspire *hosshin*. The presence of the word *wakashū* (usually used to indicate that a work is an anthology, a collection of *waka* by multiple poets, compiled by still other hands) in this title may also be modeled on its use in the titles of the *chokusenshū* (*Kokin wakashū* and its namesakes), where it gives a clear indication that the poems collected therein are Japanese poems rather than Chinese poems. But the word *wakashū* does not appear in many *shikashū* titles; it would be superfluous if it did, but for some reason it did not seem so to Senshi in this instance, if, as we assume, it was in fact she who named *Hosshin wakashū*. Like the men who gave the *chokusenshū* their names, she may have wanted to be very explicit about the fact that this was a collection of Japanese poems, and this would seem to be in keeping with her desire to explain why, in fact, she was offering *waka* rather than Sanskrit hymns or Chinese verses as a way of inducing or inspiring *hosshin*.

Senshi may also have been aware, on some level, that *hosshin* (i.e., *hotsu bodaishin*) is described in some scriptural contexts as a means whereby women may overcome the special obstacles that stand between them and Buddhahood. These obstacles, usually represented as five kinds of rebirth that women cannot experience (*goshō, itsutsu no sawari*)—the fifth of which is birth as Buddha—appear as a recurring topos in Japanese Buddhist poetry, especially by women and most frequently in

---

15. Taya Raishun, Ochō E'nichi, and Funahashi Issai, eds., *Bukkyōgaku jiten* (Kyoto: Hōzō-kan, 1955), 407–8.

daiei poems on texts that raise the issue of gender and Buddhahood.[16] Several of Senshi's poems address this topos, and it was clearly one that must have seemed most relevant to her in a collection of devotional poems that she intended to share primarily with women. *Hosshin wakashū* poem 16 is based on a passage from a text that she calls *"Tennyojōbutsukyō,"* apparently a variant of *Tennyoshingyō* (*T* no. 564), but the quoted passage is not to be found in *Tennyoshingyō*. In that sutra, however, are to be found such passages as the following:

> If women can accomplish one thing, they will be free of the female body and become sons. What is that one thing? The profound state of mind which seeks enlightenment. Why? If women awaken to the thought of enlightenment [*hotsu bodaishin*], then they will have a great and good person's state of mind, a man's state of mind, a sage's state of mind . . . If women awaken to the thought of enlightenment, then they will not be bound to the limitation of a woman's state of mind. Because they will not be limited, they will forever separate from the female sex and become sons.[17]

We have no way of knowing whether or not Senshi was familiar with this prescription for gender transformation, but we can readily see, in her poems, that she did perceive her sex as one of the factors that might block her progress toward enlightenment.[18] One sentence in the *Hosshin wakashū* preface emphasizes two circumstances of her birth: that she was born in Japan, and that when she was born she "received the form of a woman" (*deshi kōchō ni tanjō shi, mi o funyo ni uketari*). It does not refer to

---

16. The five obstructed forms of rebirth listed in various texts, including the *Lotus Sutra* (especially in the "Devadatta Chapter"—see commentary on *HSWKS* no. 36, below), are rebirth as a Brahma King (*Bonnō*), as Śakra (*Taishaku*), as Māra (*Mara*), as a Wheel-turning King (*Tenrinnō*), and as a Buddha; it is of course the last obstruction that matters most. See Kagawa Yoshio, "Bukkyō no joseikan," *Indogaku Bukkyōgaku kenkyū* 23.2 (March 1975): 45–52. One important study of Japanese responses to this and related ideas about the salvation of women is Kasahara Kazuo's *Nyonin ōjō shisō no keifu* (Tokyo: Yoshikawa Kōbunkan, 1975). Almost all of Kasahara's evidence for the Heian period is taken from literary sources, which he treats as historical documents. See also Oguri Junko, *Nyonin ōjō: Nihon shi ni okeru onna no sukui* (Tokyo: Jinbun Shoin, 1987), especially 47–56, and Paul Groner, "*The Lotus Sutra* and Saichō's Interpretation of the Realization of Buddhahood with This Very Body" in Tanabe and Tanabe, eds., *The Lotus Sutra in Japanese Culture*, 53–74.

17. Diana Paul, trans., in *Women in Buddhism: Images of the Feminine in the Mahāyāna Tradition*, 2d ed. (Berkeley: University of California Press, 1985), 175–76. See also *T* 14, p. 918.

18. See *HSWKS* poems 1, 2, 16, and 36.

her birth in the royal house, a circumstance she might have interpreted as a cause leading directly to her service as Saiin, which was perhaps the greatest of the obstacles between her and her development as a devout Buddhist. The two points that are raised both relate to her choice of *waka* as medium, but the latter also introduces the theme of the inherent weaknesses that women were taught to perceive as handicaps in their pursuit of spiritual goals—a theme that resurfaces at several points in the cycle of poems.

The preface's justification of the poet's endeavor also is based on a perception of her capacities as a woman in the society of her time, and of the special limitations placed on her capacities as a woman serving as Saiin. While others—such as her male relatives in both the imperial and the Fujiwara families—might display their devotion to Buddhism and garner merit by sponsoring the construction of "halls and pagodas" (the positive karmic effect of which is well documented in scripture), or by living the ascetic life, she could not do so. Instead, the preface says, her faith is based on the Buddha's vows to save all sentient beings—including women, whatever their handicaps may be—and she has made that faith manifest by composing poems that may be compared to those in scripture that "sing the praises" of the Buddha and his teachings. This personal religious endeavor need not cause her to depart from the "way of Japanese poetry" (*waka no michi*): if she can continue to practice this art, she need not learn to perform tantric meditations or spells or any other ritual designed to produce instantaneous Buddhahood, for the composing and sharing of these poems is tantamount to any other act of piety, and its effect may be comparably transformative. In the tantric practices referred to here generally through the phrase "*aji no mon*"—posed syntactically and symbolically against "*waka no michi*"—the sounds uttered by the human voice are understood to be representations of all phenomena, and the practitioner who takes complete control of the voice symbolically takes control of all phenomena: in short, he has a Buddha's perfect perception and a Buddha's vast power.[19] But what the preface suggests is that through the sounds represented in these poems—sounds that might of course be uttered, along with the sounds represented by the scriptural texts on which they are based—a similar result might well be achieved.

---

19. Meditation on the Sanskrit letter अ, pronounced "a" in Japanese and translated by the character 阿, was practiced, like meditation on the image of the full moon, as a means toward instantaneous attainment of Buddhahood (Yamada, "Getsurinkan to chūsei waka"). But Senshi's "*aji no mon*" probably refers to esoteric Buddhism as a whole, its various practices subsumed in this reference to a particular form of meditation.

On the basis of this point one might observe that although there is much besides time that separates Senshi from Kamakura-period and later *waka* theorists, she may still be recognized as one of the important antecedents of those who argued that a capacity for composing *waka* is identical with the capacity for attaining enlightenment, that the "way of Japanese poetry" and the "way of the Buddha" are one and the same.[20] But the argument of the *Hosshin wakashū* preface is much more particular: it is made in defense of the conception of the specific literary endeavor that is embodied in the text that follows, and it arises from a strong sense that, for a woman in Senshi's circumstances, this endeavor—the composition of these poems—was the most fitting and valuable thing that she could do.

Indeed, as the preface goes on to declare, it was Senshi's hope that the results of her endeavor—these poems—might affirm the teachings on which they were based, in emulation of Prabhūtaratna (*Tahō nyorai*), a Buddha who swears, in the *Lotus Sutra*, to prove its truth.[21] It is further hoped that this work may serve to forge a special bond that can bring about enlightenment (i.e., *kechien*) for both the poet and all those who may disparage her works: the voice in the preface prays that, like the bodhisattva Sadāparibhūta (*Jōfugyō bosatsu*)—who patiently endured the abuse of those to whom his open avowals of deep faith seemed to be no more than foolish babble—she may, through the strength of such a bond, somehow be believed even by her own detractors when she expresses her belief that they, as well as she, will all become Buddhas after all. Those who share in the forging of such a bond are assured that someday they will perfect their practice of the Buddhist way and attain complete enlightenment.

To establish *kechien* (which most literally means the tying or connecting [*kechi, musubu*] of a person to a force or cause [*en, yukari*] that will bring about his or her atttainment of Buddhahood), Senshi's contemporaries

---

20. The equation became almost a commonplace in medieval *waka* treatises. Shunzei, in *Korai fūteishō*, equates the cultivation of *waka* skills with the achievement of a quiescent mind through meditation (*shikan*)—the objective of both being superior perception of truths (see Hashimoto et al., eds., *Karonshū*, 274–75). And one of the most explicit expositions of the idea that *waka* are indistinguishable from *dhāranī* (*waka soku darani*), and are therefore also a means through which instantaneous Buddhahood can be achieved, is in Mujū Ichien's *setsuwa* collection *Shasekishū* (ca. 1279–83). See Morrell, trans., *Sand and Pebbles: The Tales of Mujū Ichien, A Voice for Pluralism in Kamakura Buddhism* (Albany: State University of New York Press, 1985), 63, 163–65. See also Yamada Shōzen, "Chūsei kōki ni okeru waka soku darani no jissen," *Indogaku Bukkyōgaku kenkyū* 16.1 (December 1967): 290–92; and Kikuchi Hitoshi, "Waka darani kō," *Denshō bungaku kenkyū* 27 (January 1983): 1–12.

21. See *T* 9, p. 32c.

undertook a wide variety of devotional practices, including some, such as the construction of holy sanctuaries, the copying of sutras, and the performance of ascetic practices or tantric rituals, to which the preface has already alluded—and which, it has been observed, she cannot undertake. *Kechien* could also arise through attendance at the reading of scriptures or lectures on them, or by bestowing charity on members of the clergy; the most powerful *kechien* would result from the act of taking Buddhist vows and becoming a priest or nun oneself. None of these courses were open to Senshi, either, and so, to bring about *kechien*, the preface implies, she wrote these poems and hoped that the act of sharing them would in itself have the effect of forming such a special bond between her and those who read them. The Chinese poems composed by the men who participated in the Kangakue were also aimed at *kechien*, but it seems that the members of that association were most concerned with sharing that bond with one another; here, on the other hand, is one woman's claim that her Japanese verses can produce the same result, and her offer to share the benefits with one and all.

"So devoted am I to the Three Jewels (*sanbō*)"—the Buddha, his teachings, and his clergy—says the voice in the preface, "that I would give up everything for their sake." But in fact, Senshi cannot as yet give up her post, or her dwelling at Murasakino or the way of life that goes with it— though time is passing. Another autumn has come, and she is yet another year older; another day is gone, and the sun now declines over the mountains that mark the western horizon. "Weeping," admits the voice, "I ponder its bright rays." Tears of frustration or tears of joy in having found and grasped the Buddha's teachings? Perhaps both. The preface ends with the date of its composition. In the "eighth month of the ninth year of the Kankō era" Senshi was forty-nine years old by the traditional Japanese count, an advanced age for a woman of her time. But another nineteen years were to pass before she would be allowed, or would allow herself, to "give up all for the sake of the Three Jewels."

In the meantime, she might make such overt demonstrations of her faith as that which is embodied in *Hosshin wakashū*, but such acts would be essentially private ones: they would not be read by any sort of public at large, nor seen by anyone likely to find them subversive of her official and ritual responsibilities, if in any sense that was what in fact they were. Rather, these poems were probably written to be shared with no larger audience than that composed by the poet's immediate circle of attendants, if that—despite the universal addresses offered in the preface. Perhaps they grew out of readings of the scripture that Senshi performed in solitude, or with one or two intimates; perhaps they and a few others then reread the cycle of sutra passages and poems repeatedly, in substitution for more open, formal devotions. But we do not really know who did read them, or how, until we reach the era in which they began to appear in the *chokusenshū,* and we can only assume (or hope) that the way they look to us when we read them today is essentially the same way that they looked to those who read them at the time that they were originally written.

The order in which the *Hosshin wakashū* poems should be read—in which there is some variance among the three bona fide copies—has been established with fair certainty by Ishihara, and it is in that order that we shall read them here.[22] The sequence, identified by the source of the passage on which each poem is based, is as follows:

> poems 1–4: on the *Shiguzeigan*[23]
> poem 5: *Hannya shingyō* ("The Heart Sutra")
> poems 6–15: on the *Fugen jūgan* (quoted from the *Kegongyō*)[24]
> poem 16: "*Tennyojōbutsukyō*" ("The Sutra on the Transformation of Women and Their Attainment of Buddhahood"[25])
> poem 17: *Nyoiringyō* (i.e., *Kanjizai Bosatsu nyoishin darani jukyō, T* no. 1081)[26]
> poem 18: *Amidakyō*
> poem 19: the "*Rishūbun*" (a section of the *Daihannya-haramittakyō*)

---

22. The poem that appears as *HSWKS* no. 53 (on a passage from the "*Fugengyō*," i.e., *Kanfugen bosatsu gyōbōgyō*) in all other copies appears as no. 19 in Shoryōbu A, which continues with the standard 54 as 20, 55 as 21, and 19–24 as 22–27, and concludes with the twenty-eight *Hokekyō* verses. Ishihara suggests that this variance may be the accidental result of a rearrangement and rebinding of the pages of Shoryōbu A. He also notes that although the edition of *HSWKS* in *Shikashū taisei* is said to be based on Shoryōbu A, the poems are presented in the sequence of Shoryōbu B—which is also the same as the sequence in the Matsudaira Bunko copy. See Ishihara, *Hosshin wakashū no kenkyū*, 66. See also Waka Shi Kenkyūkai, ed., *Shikashū taisei:* vol. 2, *Chūko* (Tokyo: Meiji Shoin, 1975), 95–97. It should be noted that none of the copies gives numbers to the poems, but modern editions do; the system used here is that used by both Ishihara and Hashimoto.

23. See n. 14, above.

24. See n. 14, above.

25. The quoted passage is not to be found in *Tennyōshingyō* (*T* no. 564) or in any other work to which this otherwise undocumented title would seem to refer.

26. "*Nyoiringyō*" would appear to refer to either *Shichishō nyoirin himitsu yōkyō* (*T* no. 1091, translated by Amoghavajra) or *Nyoirin daranikyō* (*T* no. 1080, translated by Bodhiruci), but the quoted passage is only to be found in *Kanjizai Bosatsu nyoishin darani jukyō,* a version closely related to *Nyoirin daranikyō* (translated by Yi-jing) (Ishihara, *Hosshin wakashū no kenkyū,* 106).

poems 20–21: *Ninnōkyō* (one on each fascicle, labeled *jō* and *ge*)

poem 22: *"Hongan Yakushikyō"* (perhaps *Yakushi rurikō nyorai hongan kudoku kyō, T* no. 450[27])

poem 23: *"Jumyōkyō"* (i.e., *Issai nyorai kongō jumyō daranikyō, T* no. 1135)

poem 24: *Muryōgikyō* (as the "opening" sutra of the *Lotus* triad)

poems 25–52: on passages from each of the 28 chapters (*hon*) of the *Lotus Sutra* (*Hokekyō*)

poem 53: *Fugengyō* (i.e., *Kanfugen bosatsu gyōbōgyō*, as the "closing" sutra of the *Lotus* triad)

poem 54: *Nehangyō* ("The Nirvana Sutra," *T* no. 374)

poem 55: on a passage (unlabeled as such) from the *Ke-jōyu* ("Parable of the Conjured City") chapter of the *Lotus Sutra*

In the discussion that follows, the poems will be treated sequentially in these groups: poems 1–4 (*Shiguzeigan*); poem 5; poems 6–15 (*Fugen jūgan*); poems 16–23 (on various texts); poems 24–53 (*Hokekyō* and its "opening and closing" sutras); poems 54–55 (concluding poems). Other sequences that are thematically or otherwise linked will also be treated in subgroups within these larger groupings.

Shiguzeigan: The Four Vast Vows

(1) *shujō muben zeigando*
Sentient beings are numberless: I vow to save them all.

tare to naku hitotsu ni nori no ikada nite
    kanata no kishi ni tsuku yoshimogana
How I wish there were a way for all to ride together,
    without distinctions,
        the dharma a raft that carries us to the opposite shore!

---

27. No passage corresponding exactly to that used by Senshi is to be found in the existing translations of the Yakushi sutras. However, the same text is quoted from a work referred to as *"Zuigan Yakushi kyō"* in the "Torinomai" chapter of *Eiga monogatari* (*NKBT* 76, 153). Matsumura Hiroji has suggested that this *"Zuigan Yakushi kyō"* may have been a name for the now lost *Yakushi rurikō kyō* translated by Hui-jian of the Liu-Sung (fl. mid-5th century), and Ishihara tentatively posits that this work may be Senshi's source (Ishihara, *Hosshin wakashū no kenkyū*, 118). The passage quoted by Senshi does closely resemble the exposition of Bhaiṣajya-guru's seventh vow in Xuan-zang's translation (see the *Yakushi rurikō nyorai hongan kudoku kyō; T* 14, no. 450, pp. 401c, 405a-b).

(2) *bonnō mube zeigandan*
Afflictions [obstacles to enlightenment] are numberless: I
vow to eliminate them all.

kazoubeki kata mo nakeredo mi ni chikaki
    mazu wa itsutsu no sawari narikeru
There is no way to count them all, but those that are
    closest to me
    are certainly those Five Obstructions.

(3) *hōmon mujin zeiganchi*
The Buddhist teachings are inexhaustible: I vow to know
them all.

ikani shite tsukushite shiran
    satoru koto irukotogataki kado to kikedomo
Somehow I will learn all there is to know,
    though they say it is difficult to gain enlightenment,
    difficult to enter the gate to it.

(4) *mujō bodai zeiganshō*
The ultimate form of enlightenment: I vow to attain it.

kokonoshina sakihiraku naru hachisuha no
    ue no ue naru mi to mo narabaya
Of the nine classes of lotus that are said to bloom,
    let my rebirth take place upon the very highest!

Each of the *Shiguzeigan* is expressed in seven characters; the formulations
of the first three bodhisattva vows are syntactically repetitive, and the
fourth is a slight variation of the same syntax. In each case, the poet finds
ways to render major elements of the formulation into language that fits
the *waka*, while she restates or interprets the vows in more personal
terms. The verb (the last element in each of the vow formulations) in the
first vow is the character read *do*, construed in the first *waka* as the figurative *watasu*, "convey to, cause to cross (to the 'opposite shore')," i.e.,
"cause to be saved from worldly suffering and achieve the state of Buddhahood." The poem is an elaboration of this *do* as it is understood in
Buddhist contexts: it prompts *nori no ikada*, "the dharma raft," the Buddhist teachings symbolized as a vehicle that bears the faithful across troubled waters to *kanata no kishi*, "the opposite shore."[28] *Tsuku*, "arrive at/

---

28. The figure expressed here as *kanata no kishi* is often rendered as *higan*; its association
with *nori no ikada* is conventional. *Nori no ikada* is also closely related to *nori no ukigi*,

reach (the opposite shore)," marks the completion of the motion of *do/watasu*, while *yoshimogana* (literally, "how I wish there were a means [to do it]") marks the utterance as the poem-speaker's own fervent wish.

And who is the poem-speaker? To the reader who has already been made conscious of the identity of the author of the cycle (by the context in which it is presented), the voice may be unmistakably Senshi's. If it is the preface that has inculcated that consciousness and created that context, then the voice that utters the first poem (and most or all the poems) in the cycle can certainly be heard as the same voice as that which announces its goals in the preface. Most readers will take this voice to be Senshi's. At the same time, however, the first poem *can* be understood to be an utterance by the same anonymous and genderless bodhisattva who utters the vows. But as soon as the reader reads the second poem, this possibility recedes, and even the reader who would set context and personality aside will have to recognize that it is the voice of a woman that is asserting itself in poem 2. Senshi does not deliver her poems in an anonymous or genderless voice, nor does she read the scriptural passages that are their foundation as an anonymous or genderless reader, but as a woman, as herself. She reiterates these bodhisattva vows in terms that are very much her own.

Thus, in the second vow, "*bonnō*" could be broadly construed as "(forms of) ignorance/illusion," and in poem 2 these are acknowledged to be numberless (*kazoubeki kata mo nakeredo*): but the ones that are of the greatest concern to the poem-speaker (*mi ni chikaki*, "relevant to my self") are a specific "Five Obstructions" (*itsutsu no sawari*)—unmistakably, the five forms of rebirth, including rebirth as Buddhas, that women cannot experience. What has happened here is that the word *bonnō*, generally understood as "afflictions" or "evil passions" that obstruct or divert the mind from perception of the truth and prevent progress toward enlightenment, has been understood rather as a category of "evils" that block aspirations toward Buddhahood, the most serious blocks to women being the notion that they are, by their very nature as women, impeded in the path toward Buddhahood itself. The introduction of this idea in turn casts new light back on poem 1: the wish for inclusiveness, that "all,

---

the Buddhist teachings figured as a floating log, as in Senshi's Mitarashigawa tortoise poem (see above) and *HSWKS* no. 51, both of which are based on the passage in the "*Myōshōgon bon*" of the *Lotus* (*T* 9, p. 60) that introduces the figure. The frequent use of such figures in Buddhist poetry was abetted by the capacity of the word *nori* not only to mean "the teachings" (as here), but also to appear as a form of the verb *noru*, "to ride (on a vehicle)," which in turn can be associated with the common figuring (in the *Lotus* and elsewhere) of "the teachings" as "vehicles" (*norimono*); see, for example, *HSWKS* no. 27.

without distinction" may ride "together" on the raft, may refer specifically
to the hope that women may not be excluded; the poet's response to the
vow-text is a restatement of it that asks, hopefully, "Will I—can I—be one
of those who will be saved?" The woman who asks this question knows
that she can believe the answer to be "yes"; she knows about the example
of the Nāga girl in the "Devadatta" chapter of the *Lotus Sutra*, who proved
how easily the obstacles faced by women could be overcome. (See *Hosshin
wakashū* no. 36, below.) Yet, such questioning of the real terms of "universal salvation" recurs as topos and theme in *waka* discourse between
women (or others speaking for them) and the texts and institutions of
Buddhism—even when those same texts and institutions, or competing
ones, teach that Buddhahood can be attained by all who have sincere
faith.[29]

Poem 3 can be read as a continuation of that same discourse. Achiev-
ing the goal of learning "all the teachings" (*hōmon mujin*, which parallels
shujō muben and *bonnō mube*) is said to be difficult for all, but how much

---

29. The tenacity of this *waka* topos in the face of ample doctrinal and other kinds of
refutation is a testament to its gravity in the minds of medieval women, who perhaps
saw it more as a symbol of their treatment as inferiors in certain social spheres than as
a factor that would determine the condition of their future lives. In a poem by Izumi
Shikibu (*Shin senzai wakashū* no. 894) the "five obstructions" topos comes into play
with another institutional exclusion of women—in this case, the rule that they could
not enter the monastic precincts on Mount Hie, the Tendai headquarters northeast of
the capital:

When a priest passed her house carrying a maidenflower (*ominaeshi*), she asked
him where he was going, and when he said, "I am taking this flower as an
offering for the *nenbutsu* rite on Mount Hie (*Hie no yama no nenbutsu no tatebana ni
namu motemakaru*)," she wrote this and attached it to the flower:

*na ni shi owaba itsutsu no sawari aru mono o
urayamashiku mo noboru hana ka na*
If this truly is its name, it faces the Five Obstructions, and yet
how enviable this flower that mounts the heights!

(*SKT* 1, 618.) Obviously, this poem is as much concerned with the poetic sug-
gestiveness of the name of the flower and the possibility of figuring it as if it had
human female attributes, as it is with the doctrinal notion of the obstructions, but the
exclusion theme is compounded in the particular context established by the
kotobagaki. That compounding is also involved in the double significance of the verb
noboru, which refers both to "going up the mountain" and "going up onto the altar as
an offering." The first five-syllable section of the poem (*na ni shi owaba*) also echoes
Ariwara Narihira's famous (and frequently imitated) query addressed to the "capital
bird" (*miyakodori*) in *Ise monogatari* section 9/*Kokin wakashū* no. 411.

Another pairing of "the five obstructions" and "maidenflower" occurs in a poem by
Fujiwara Mototoshi (1060–1142; *Mototoshi shū* no. 115). A certain woman, says the
kotobagaki, wanted to send an *ominaeshi* as an offering for the "nonstop *nenbutsu*" (*futai*

more difficult will it be for a woman, especially a woman in Senshi's position? The poem restates the firm resolve as one colored by a sense of striving against great odds. The links between topic-text and poem are firm: the verb *chi* (in Sino-Japanese reading) prompts *shiran* in the *waka*, while the vow's figurative *hōmon* suggests "entry" as well as the literalized "gate" (*kado*) in the poem. But tension is created when the absolute resolve of the vow-text is restated and personalized.

Poem 4 is also a personalized restatement. In the vow-text, the object of the verb *shō* (i.e., *satoru*—"realize [enlightenment]"—in final position, as in the other vows) is expressed in the first four characters, whereas in the preceding vows the first two characters identifed the object and the second two functioned adverbially, with "*mu* + (x)" indicating absolute inclusiveness; here, *mujō* is a modifier ("ultimate") of *bodai*, "enlightenment." *Mujō bodai* is one of the translations of *anuttara-samyak-sambodhi*, but the particular form of "ultimate enlightenment" for which the poet prays is permanent rebirth in glory on one of the Lotus Thrones in

---

no nenbutsu, i.e., *fudan nenbutsu*) in the eighth month (an autumn month with which the maidenflower was closely associated) and asked Mototoshi to compose a poem for her to submit with it. He wrote:

> *wa ga gotoku itsutsu no sawari aru hana o*
> *ikaga hachisu no mi to wa nasubeki*
> How can this flower, which, like me, faces the Five Obstructions,
>   be made into a being who can be born anew upon a lotus?

(*SKT* 3, 470.) In other words, the poem asks, if this flower, though impeded in the same way as human women are, has a chance to participate in a rite designed to produce eventual rebirth in the Pure Land, can it indeed overcome those obstructions (through that participation) and receive that reward? (As presented by the *kotobagaki*, this and Izumi Shikibu's poem seem to suggest that there may have been a custom of sending *ominaeshi* to Hie rites as substitutes for or representatives of real women.)

In the *Shakkyōka* section of *Shin senzai wakashū*, Shikibu's *ominaeshi* poem is paired with another *itsutsu no sawari* poem (the *kotobagaki* says "*dai shirazu*" [topic unknown], but the topical association between the two poems is clear) by Kianmon'in (d. 1357), consort of the emperor Kōgon (*Shin senzai wakashū* no. 895):

> *tanomu zo yo itsutsu no sawari fukaku to mo sutenu*
> *hotoke no chikai hitotsu o*
> How I rely on it—the Buddha's single vow,
>   which nonetheless does not entirely rid me of the Five Obstructions.

(*SKT* 1, 618.) This poem deliberately poses five against one—the one being most probably the thirty-fifth vow of Amida Buddha (according to the *Muryōjukyō* listing), which insures the rebirth of all women in his Pure Land: in other words, the poem poses one doctrinal tradition of exclusion, that of women from Buddhahood per se, against another doctrinal tradition of inclusion, that of women among those who can attain eternal rebirth in paradise (*ōjō*).

Amida's Pure Land. *Ue no ue* directly transforms *mujō*, while the de-
siderative *narabaya* ("*I want to become* [a being that is on the highest of the
highest of the Nine Lotus Thrones that are said to bloom there]") is an
explicit personalizing element. The preface offered the prayer that all
readers of this text would be "inspired with the desire to reach Amida's
paradise and ultimately be reborn there on one of the Nine Lotus
Thrones." Here, recasting the bodhisattva's vow, the poet affirms this as
her own goal as well.

Hannya shingyō: The Heart Sutra

(5) *shiki soku ze kū, kū soku ze shiki,*
    ju sō gyō shiki, yakubu nyo ze[30]
"Form is emptiness, emptiness is form;
the same is true of feelings, perceptions, impulses and
consciousness."[31]

yoyo o hete tokikuru nori wa ōkaredo
    kore zo makoto no kokoro narikeru
The teachings that have been propounded through the
ages are many,
but this one is truly the heart of them all.

In many *waka* (and, later, *renga*) sequences, whether designed by the poet
or by later editors, remarkable poems that draw attention to themselves
with bold statements, unusual diction, or other techniques are deliberately juxtaposed with more straightforward poems. Whether deliberately
so arranged or not, some sequences of poems in *Hosshin wakashū* also
display such alternation. After the explicitly personalized and rather exhil-
arated utterances of the preceding four poems, poem 5 is relatively simple: its chief feature is the transparent rendering of *shin* (heart), from the
title of the sutra, as *kokoro* (also heart) in the *waka*. The line quoted from
the sutra is one of its most familiar, a quintessential statement of the
Prajñā doctrine of nonsubstantiality, and the poem praises this line as the
embodiment of a teaching that forms the core of all Buddhist doctrine.
Nori, "teaching" (doctrine, dharma) has returned, but not as figured in
poem 1; here, it could mean the sutra as a whole as well as the passage
(the quotation) that conveys its essence. (Hence, "there are many sutras
that have come down to us, but this is the one that tells the essential

---

30. *T* 8, p. 848c.

31. Edward Conze, trans., *Buddhist Wisdom Books* (New York: Harper and Row/Harper
    Torchbooks, 1958), 81.

truth.") *Kore zo* points emphatically to the quoted line, creating a close link between the poem and quotation that is of another order than the *shin/kokoro* link; thus, while the statement of the poem is not directly related to the statement of the topic-quotation, the language of the poem engages the text that precedes it in intimate play. And, perhaps, the certainty of *kore zo* suggests a greater clarity of perception than does the wishful, even guarded language of any of the preceding poems. If so, that clarity may be a reflection of the unequivocal language of the sutra-passage and the liberating doctrine it sets forth.

Fugen jūgan: The Ten Vows of Samantabhadra

(6) *Raikyō shobutsu*: I shall do homage to all the Buddhas.

Through the marvelous power of my vow to lead a most
    excellent life
I shall appear before all the Buddhas;
My one body shall become as many bodies as there are grains
    of dust on the earth,
And each one shall do reverence to each and every Buddha.[32]

kimi dani mo chiri no naka ni mo arawareba
    tatsu to iru to zo iyamawarubeki
Even you, Samantabhadra, would appear even amidst
    the dust to do so,
        so surely I, whatever I may do, must in doing so
        do honor to the Buddhas.

(7) *Shōsan nyorai*: I shall praise the Tathāgata[s].

With a voice as vast as an ocean that sounds all sounds,
Producing numberless wondrous words,
I shall sing through all the kalpas of time to come
In praise of the ocean of merit in the depths of the Buddha's
    heart.

omou ni mo iu ni mo amaru fukasa nite
    koto mo kokoro mo oyobarenu ka na
Beyond thinking, beyond speaking, these depths are still
    greater,
        and neither my words nor my heart can plumb them.

---

32. See *T* 10, no. 293, p. 847a–48b for the topic-texts of *HSWKS* poems 6–15.

(8) *Kōshu kuyō*: I shall make offerings everywhere.

Using my far-reaching correct perceptions
And my great faith in all the Buddhas of the Three Ages
I shall, through the great power of these vows,
Make all manner of offerings to all the Tathāgatas.

sashinagara miyo no hotoke ni tatematsuru
    haru saku hana mo aki no momiji mo
Let me offer them all to the Buddhas of the Three Ages:
    the flowers that bloom in spring, the colored leaves of
    autumn.

(9) *Sange gosshō*: I shall do penance for evil karma.

All the bad karma I created in the past
Through limitless greed, ill will, ignorance and anger,
All caused by my body, my words, and my mind:
Now, here, I repent it all.

toshigoro zo tsukisezarikeru wagami yori
    hito no tame made nagekitsuzukuru[33]
My lament is not only for my own self, with its sins un-
    abating as years go by,
        but goes on to grieve for the sake of others as well.

(10) *Zuiki kudoku*: I shall rejoice in the merits of others.

All sentient beings of the Ten Directions,
Those in the Two Vehicles,[34] those who have learned all and
    those who have not,
And all the Tathāgatas and bodhisattvas, too:
I shall praise and rejoice in the merits of them all.

chikakute mo tōku kikite mo konokata wa
    nagorinaku koso arawarenikere

---

33. In all three extant copies of HSWKS the poem begins "*rukoroso* るころそ," which makes no sense, but Hashimoto has suggested that "*ru-*" る is a miscopying of the character for "*toshi*" 年 (SKT 3, 890).

34. "Those in the Two Vehicles" refers to *śrāvaka* and *pratyekabuddha*, practitioners and devotees of Hīnayana teachings.

From near and far, knowing and unknowing—
  they have all appeared here before me![35]

(11) *Shōten bōrin*: I shall invite others to turn the Dharma
Wheel.

All those in all the Ten Directions who are a light unto the
  world,
Those who will be first to attain ultimate Bodhi:
I now invite them all
To turn the superior and wondrous Dharma Wheel.

nochi made mo hirometeshigana
  kaeru to te nori no chigiri o musubiokisue
I want to spread it even into the future,
  so that when I leave this life I shall have established
  strong bonds with the dharma.

(12) *Shōbutsu jūse*: I shall urge the Buddhas to remain in
this world.

If the Buddhas should wish to display their attainment of
  Nirvana
I shall fervently entreat and encourage them
And pray that they may remain in this world for as many
  kalpas as there are particles of dust in it
To save and give succor to all sentient beings.

minahito no hikari o augu sora no tsuki
  nodoka ni terase kumogakuresede
O moon in the sky whose light is sought by one and all:
  shine gently and do not hide behind the clouds.

(13) *Jōzui butsugaku*: I shall always follow the example of
the Buddhas.

Following the example of all the Tathāgatas,
I shall fulfill these vows in perfect practice,

---

35. Poem 10 appears here as reconstructed by Hashimoto, who has tried to resolve
discrepancies in the forms in which it appears in the various copies and early modern
editions. The poem remains almost indecipherable, and for this reason I will not
attempt to discuss it in detail; the English version is offered as a gloss on Hashimoto's
reconstruction.

And I shall make offerings to all the Tathāgatas of the past
And to those of the present in all the Ten Directions.

ikani shite nori o tamotamu
    yo ni fureba neburi mo samenu yume no kanashisa
Somehow I will uphold the dharma!
    As long as I am in this world, I am trapped in a sad dream
    from which I do not wake.

(14) *Gōjun shujō*: I shall adapt to the lives of sentient
beings.

I shall adapt to the lives of sentient beings,
And through the very end of time
I shall constantly repeat these great practices
Until I attain perfect, ultimate Bodhi.

ureshiki mo tsuraki mo koto ni wakarenu wa
    hito ni shitagau kokoro narikeri
Since there are such differences between those who are
    happy and those who suffer still,
    I commit myself to adaptation to the needs of each.

(15) *Fukai ekō*: I shall direct all, everywhere, into the right
path.

I shall transfer all the merit
From the practice of these excellent deeds to others
And I pray that all those who are drowning in their sufferings
May straightway go to the land of the Buddha of Endless
    Light.

kakubakari sokoi mo shiranu wagayami ni
    shizuman hito o ukabeteshigana
I want to set afloat all those who are about to drown
    in darkness whose depth they cannot know.

Each of the ten vows is expressed first in a four-character encapsulation
and then in a verse of two couplets of seven-character lines.[36] The *waka*

---

36. I have transliterated only the four-character encapsulations, the readings for which
are fairly standardized. For that matter, I have not transliterated any of the other

responses to these vows adopt various stances, but in most cases the poem-speaker says, "I, too, will do what you, bodhisattva, say you will do in your vow." Thus as a group these ten poems constitute a reiteration of the bodhisattva's determination to bring about universal enlightenment and salvation—which is also the professed aim of the cycle—but in that reiteration the poet imposes a more personal voice that speaks from a less abstract position. The transformations of discrete elements of the vow-texts into elements of the *waka* texts accompany and signal this change.

In the first vow-text, *setsujin shin* and *setsujin butsu* are in parallel position at the end of each of the lines in the second couplet, indicating that the numberless manifestations of the vow-sayer will worship an equal number of numberless Buddhas. In poem 6, these two *jin* have become the *chiri* of *chiri no naka ni mo arawareba*: the vow-speaker is praised for his willingness to manifest himself "even in this dust-sullied world," and, in awe, the poem-speaker can only promise to do homage with similar determination. The words "appear" and "do honor" in the poem (*arawar[eba]* and *iyamaw[arubeki]*) come straight from the vow (the latter from the *raikyō* of the four-character form as well as from the reappearance of *rai* in the last seven-character line), whereas *"tatsu to iru to"*—which means, literally, "whether standing or sitting," and is an example of the simplest form of parallel syntax conventionally employed in *waka*—is a freer interpretation of *hen* ("in many places").

The meritorious deed averred in the second vow is "singing in praise" (*san*), and the composition of the *waka* in response to it (no. 7) is part of a similar project, the "singing in praise" of the Buddhist teachings that the whole cycle embodies. The vow-speaker will sing in a voice that fills the world as does the roaring sea, but the poem-speaker wonders whether her voice will resound as fully. The words for the praiseworthy "depth" (*shin*) of the Buddha's "heart" (*shin*) both find their way into the poem as *fukasa* and *kokoro*, but they are recast: the dimensions of the Buddha's praiseworthiness, and of the project, are so vast that the poem-speaker worries whether her mind can perceive them and whether the words she employs in her "songs" will be equal to the task. The language of the vow has adroitly been turned to a comment on the poem-speaker's own related project. As if to balance this movement "outward" from the context of the

---

HSWKS topic-texts except the first five, which also have standardized readings. (Some selected phrases are transliterated in my discussions of the quotations and poems.) As previously noted, it is quite difficult to reconstruct the Heian reading of scriptural passages such as those quoted at length here (which may well have been intended for oral reproduction), except where texts are provided with *kana* glosses and/or the special kinds of punctuation used to render Chinese as "readable" Japanese. No *HSWKS* texts offer such apparatuses.

vow to the context of the poem-cycle and its project, the poem itself plays with an inverted parallelism: "thinking" and "saying" (*omou, iu*), at the beginning of the poem, point to "the contents of the heart/mind" (*kokoro*, the fruits of "thinking") and to the "words" (*koto*) that manifest those thoughts (*omou // iu; koto // kokoro*).

Poem 8 appears to be a less complex response: the poet's form of offering (*kuyō*) to the Buddhas of the past, present, and future will be cherry blossoms in spring and *momiji* in autumn—modest commodities, easily obtained in their season. But, since these blossoms and leaves are the most potent emblems not only of their seasons but also of the poems that those seasons yield, this poem may also say, "I shall present these and all the poems that I write as offerings to the Buddhas, too." And the syntactic parallelism of *haru saku hana mo aki no momiji mo* does more than give this poem its balanced shape: it also draws a formal link to the two preceding poems and the parallelisms that shape them.

The fourth vow-text begins with an unequivocal "I," and the poem echoes this with *wagami* ("my own self"); its first word, *toshigoro* ("many years") is also derived from the second character in the vow, *jaku/mukashi*, and its only verb, *nagekitsuzukuru*, expressed in the final five syllables, is an interpretation of the last word of the vow, *sange* ("[I] repent"—also the first word of the four-character encapsulation). In adopting the vow as her own, however, the poet introduces a reference to her own state, the specific situation that has caused her to be sinful. She then expands the act of contrition beyond sorrow and penance for her own sin and extends it to "others" (*hito*): her companions in the Saiin establishment, similarly limited in their Buddhist pieties (and accepting those limitations on her account), or perhaps "*all* other people." The structural feature of the poem that expresses this extension—its X *yori* Y *made* ([beginning] from X [and extending] to Y) formulation—may derive from the two characters in the vow, *yu* and *jū*, both of which might be read "*yori*" but which function in the vow-text to mark the *source* and *cause* of the sins repented by the speaker rather than to delineate an extent or extension (which is further marked in the poem by -*tsuzuk[uru]*, "continue"). This particular transformation may represent a misreading or misinterpretation of the grammatical function of these characters, but the misreading or misinterpretation may be deliberate, a subtle but intentional linkage of a graphic element of the topic-text with a semantic facet of the poem-text. The poem also responds to the vow-text by *not* introducing a word to match "*akugyō*" ("bad karma") in the vow, or even by interpreting it with a word like "*tsumi*" or something similar; thus, even though the poem reinterprets the vow, it literally shares its focus of concern and need not reproduce that central element. Such nonreproduction of elements in the topic-text is actually a means of simultaneously reiterating and transforming it.

The key interpretive word in poem 11 is *hirometeshigana*, "I want to spread [it]": what will be spread is "the dharma" (*nori*), just as it is spread in the action of those who are said to turn the "Dharma Wheel" (*hōrin*, or "*bōrin*" in the conventional encapsulation). The poem-speaker will herself be one of those that turn the wheel, thereby "inviting" others to do so, even after her own departure from this world. Whereas the vow-text seems to be uttered into and for the present world, the poem expresses hope for effects that will be everlasting. *Kaeru to te* (literally, "speaking of 'return'" or "upon returning") is open to several interpretations. It may look forward to the poem-speaker's reversion from one mode of life to another (such as Senshi's projected release from her Kamo duties and her return to "normal" life), but it may also refer to the constant turning and returning of the Dharma Wheel, coming back again and again to find the poem-speaker ever more deeply committed to her faith.

In the poetic response (no. 12) to the seventh vow-text, the plural Buddhas (*shobutsu*) of the vow-text have become one, represented by the light of the full moon toward which "one and all" (*minahito*, perhaps a rendering of "all sentient beings," *issai sho shujō*, in the last line of the vow-text) cast their eyes. This moon, like the many Buddhas addressed by the vow-speaker, is literally asked not to die—not to extinguish its light under the cover of clouds (*kumogakuresede: kumogakur[u]* is a euphemism for "die," literally "hide in the clouds"). The poem, a fervent request addressed directly to the Buddha-moon, is not a statement of intent, as is the vow-text, but an enactment based on a poetic interpretation of that intent. The interpolation of a conventional *waka* topos—pleading that the moon not hide or be hidden (as in Narihira's "*akanaku ni . . .*"[37])—distances the poem from the scriptural text, but it is precisely that interpolation, as well as the directness of the form of address, that mark the poem as a wholly new and significantly personalized poetic utterance.

There is a similar distance between the text of the eighth vow and poem 13. "Somehow," vows the poem-speaker (employing rhetoric that parallels the similarly qualified reiteration in poem 3) she will "uphold the dharma" (*ikani shite nori o tamotamu*), thus emulating the vow-speaker, who will "fulfill these vows in perfect practice" (*shushū fugen enmangyō*). At the same time, introducing the conventional figure of "the dream from which I do not wake," the poem-speaker bemoans the conditions of her present life (*yo ni fureba . . .*) that make it so hard for her to practice the teachings. The poem reveals doubt about its speaker's capacity to realize the lofty intentions expressed in the bodhisattva's vows: she cannot wholly appropriate them, but will take what part of them she can and

---

37. See part one, n. 27, above.

hope to do her best with them. This partial appropriation is paralleled in the relationship of the poem and the text of which it is a "partial" rendering.

On the surface, poem 14 appears to be a much more complete rendering of its vow-text, a straightforward reiteration and mimed fulfillment of the bodhisattva's promise to adapt (*jun* in the vow, *shitagau* in the poem) to the needs of others; for this reading, the implied "I" of the vow-text must remain the same "I" of the *waka* utterance. (Otherwise, the poem can be read as one referring to any bodhisattva: "*He* or *she* therefore commits himself/herself to adaptation to the needs of each.") For this poet, however, the distinction between those "with reason to be glad" and "those who suffer still" (*ureshiki mo tsuraki mo*) may be the distinction between those who fully and openly devote themselves to Buddhism and those who cannot. If so, she is one of the latter, for she must herself "adapt" to the expectations of others even if they are counter to her private goals. So the poem-speaker may also be saying something like this: "There are those who make me happy as well as those who make things difficult for me; it is for that reason that I adapt myself to each (*hito ni shitagau kokoro narikeri*)."[38]

Nonetheless, the same poem-speaker says in her reiteration of the tenth and last vow, "I want to do what I can to save those who suffer." In the vow-text the suffering ones are "drowning beings" (*chindeki sho shujō*), but the bodhisattva says he will "transfer his limitless excellent merit" (*mube shōbuku kai ekō*) to them in order to speed them toward Amitābha's paradise (*muryōkōbussetsu*). In poem 15, it is in bottomless darkness, the opposite of "endless light" (*muryōkō*), that the suffering sink. The light of rescue shines elsewhere, and the poem-speaker herself may not yet have seen it: *wagayami* may be both "their darkness" and "my darkness." Yet, the poem-speaker would propel others toward the light, and the means of rescue she would employ—the transfer of merit, identified as one of the objects of the entire project—is the same means employed by the vow-speaker.

Tennyo jōbutsugyō: The Sutra on the Transformation of Women and Their Attainment of Buddhahood

---

38. My reading of this poem takes *-nu* in *wakarenu* as the *shūshikei* (final form) of *nu*, a perfective suffix, but Robert N. Huey has suggested an alternate reading: if this *-nu* is the *rentaikei* (attributive form) of *zu*, a negative suffix, and if *koto ni wakar[u]* is taken as a form of *koto ni su*, "to distinguish [one thing from another]," the poem may mean "something like 'By not distinguishing between the happy and the suffering, in this way do I adapt to the needs of people'" (Robert N. Huey, private communication).

(16) "All the evil karma from previous lives will be extinguished, and she will certainly attain Great Bodhisattvahood; in the end, her female body will be transformed, and
she will reach the Ultimate Way."[39]

toriwakite tokareshi nori ni ainureba
    mi mo kaetsubeku kiku zo ureshiki
Since I have encountered this teaching given specially for me,
    it is certain that my body will be transformed—what joy
    to hear it!

In previous poems (nos. 1, 5, 11, 13), nori meant "the dharma," the Buddhist teachings as a whole, but in no. 16 nori is a specific "teaching," the
idea that by various means (unspecified in the quoted passage) a woman
can cut herself off from her past and its determinations (which have
produced her present womanhood) and attain the most advanced spiritual state, and that, by the same means, she can change physically from
female to male and thus—having circumvented the Five Obstructions—
qualify for Buddhahood. (As noted above, the best known transformation
is that of the Nāga girl, described in the "Devadatta" chapter of the Lotus
Sutra, and the miracle of transformation will again be marveled at in the
poem [36] that responds to a passage from that chapter; see also 47 and
48.) The first two clauses (possibly couplets) of the present passage—the
exact source and context of which, as noted above, cannot be identified—
are each of five characters, while the third and fourth each have four
characters. The pattern, if such it is, suggests that the passage could be an
amalgamation of couplets from two different verse-passages in some version of the "Transformation" sutra. In any case, the poem remains closely
linked to the quoted passage, to which nori may refer even as it refers to
the content of the passage and of the scripture in which it appeared. This
"teaching" of which the speaker has had the good fortune to learn (she
has literally "met" it [ainureba], as worthy teachers and great opportunities
are said to have been "met" with) is one that the Buddha has taken special
pains to provide and explicate (toriwakite tokareshi nori), and it is extraordinary, for, this recipient believes, it is given especially to women so that
they may have some hope of ultimate salvation. Now, the poem-speaker
says—in a voice that is clearly that of a woman rejoicing in such hope—
having encountered this scripture and its message (an encounter re-
enacted now in the text itself), she knows that her physical form will
change (mi mo kaetsubeku), that the conditions of her present life that
distance her from the attainment of Buddhahood will be altered, and that

---

39. See n. 25, above.

she will surely realize her highest goals. The romantic encounters of men and women that transform their lives and the way they see their world were often recorded in poems that use forms of the verb *au* to mark their meeting; here, the poet has found new resonance for this poetic language of encounter. The sense of certainty suggested in *kaetsubeku* may echo the adverbials (*masa ni . . .* and *hatashite* in *kundoku* reading) in the second and third clauses of the quotation, establishing another kind of link between the passage and the poem that also carries the cyclical discourse into a brief interval of assurance.

Nyoiringyō: The Wish-Granting Wheel Sutra

(17) "Amida Buddha shall display his body, and you shall see the Pure Land and its myriad splendors."[40]

kokonagara kashiko no kazari arawaruru toki zo
    kokoro no gotoku narikeru[41]
Though it happens here in this world, when the glories of that land appear,
    my heart's great wish seems to be fulfilled.

Amidakyō: The Amida Sutra.

(18) The lotuses in those lakes are as big as carriage wheels.
    There are lotuses of blue color and blue light,
    Lotuses of yellow color and yellow light,
    Lotuses of red color and red light,
    Lotuses of white color and white light,
    And their perfume is wondrously strong.[42]

iroiro no hachisu kakayaku ikemizu ni
    kanau kokoro ya sumite miyuran
Does my heart appear to be as pure as those pure waters
    that shine with all the colors of the lotuses?

The speaker of the *Nyoiringyō* passage is the Bodhisattva Avalokiteśvara (identified in this context as *"Kanjizai bosatsu"*), affirming and praising

---

40. *T* 20, no. 1081, p. 197a. See n. 26, above.

41. Shoryōbu A reads *"mi-na-u-ko kashiko no usa mo arawaruru . . ."* みなうこかしこの うさもあらはる丶 , which is unintelligible. Shoryōbu B and the Shimabara copy agree; their version is that given here.

42. *T* 12, no. 366, p. 347a.

Amida's promises to those who place their faith in him. The quoted passage does not specify the conditions under which Amida and the glories of the Pure Land will be revealed; in the sutra, however, these are promised as the result of chanting that text itself.[43] The speaker of the poem proclaims that though she is still "here," in the present and real conditions of this world (*kokonagara*), she too can see the same fabulous splendors (*shuju shōgon* in the sutra-passage, *[kashiko no] kazari* in the poem) that are "over there." We do not know by what means she has reached that level of perception; something, however, makes them appear (*arawar[u]*)—perhaps meditation, perhaps an intense reading of a text that describes them vividly, such as that which is the source of the quoted passsage. The result is a bridging of the gap between "here" and "there": it is as if the experience of a vision of the Pure Land is tantamount to being in it. In the sutra, immediately before the passage reproduced here, Avalokiteśvara says, "Good sons, you need have no fear. All that you seek and pray for shall be granted to you," and the addition of the lines that follow yields "You shall see the Pure Land and its myriad splendors *just as they are described in this scripture* (*nyo kyō kō setsu*)." The poem's "*kokoro no gotoku narikeru*"—literally, "it is now just as it is in my heart" ("as I wished/imagined it to be")—would seem to partake of these parts of the topic-text, too, although they are not actually part of the *dai*.[44]

The poet struggles with the *tanka* form to express all this. There is no caesura in this poem where one is usually to be found (in *waka* in general, including those in *Hosshin wakashū*), either after the first seven-syllable group or the second five-syllable group. Instead, *kazari*, at the end of the first seven, must be read as the grammatical subject of *arawar[uru]*, a verb that comprises the second five; its attributive form, however, forces the reader onward to the word *toki*, making all that comes before it a modifying clause. It is unusual to find such modifiers bridging points in the thirty-one-syllable sequence where syntactic breaks usually occur. The result is a *waka* that reads more like a conventional sentence than most *waka* do, one that gives the impression of the poet's willingness to resist the exigencies of form in order to forge a poem with overt links to its topic-text.[45]

---

43. *T* 20, no. 1081, p. 196c.

44. See *T* 20, p. 197a. The word *nyoishin*, "just as it is conceived in the mind/heart," is also part of the full title of the work from which the *dai* is taken. See n. 26, above.

45. When read aloud, the repetition of "k-" sounds in this poem is very striking. Alliteration of this kind, and to this degree, does not occur anywhere else in the cycle as conspicuously as it does here, although it is perhaps not an accident that the same sound is dominant in the following poem as well.

The splendors of the Pure Land that were seen in poem 17 are drawn in fuller detail in the passage quoted next from Kumārajīva's translation of the *Amidakyō*. (The passage comes from a verse section of the preface to the sutra: the Buddha is describing the Pure Land to his disciple Śāriputra.) The poem, however, is no simple celebration of the passage or of the sutra that contains it or of the Pure Land ideal that it propounds. It begins with a rather obvious pun: the many colors (*iro*) of lotuses and light catalogued in the quoted passage prompt "*iroiro no*," "the many and varied," describing *hachisu* (lotuses). But the poem-speaker wants to ask whether her spiritual purity can possibly be compared with that of the pure waters in which those lotuses are said to grow.[46] Within the cyclical context this speaker, who wonders how her inner self (her *kokoro*) appears to others, is clearly the same woman who, in the immediately preceding poems, was rejoicing in her visualization of the Pure Land and in the certainty that the gender-based obstacles to Buddhahood could be overcome, but here she is far less certain of her spiritual attainments. To express this, the poet shifts the descriptive focus from the lotus flowers and the light they emit to the water of the lotus ponds—an inherent element of the scene not explicitly named in the sutra-passage. By doing so she initiates a discourse on purity, asking rhetorically whether she herself can ever be compared to that pure water. If we think of the poem-speaker as identical with the poet, the question takes on some irony: a woman whose very purpose in life is to cultivate ritual purity as defined in one religious tradition is asking whether she can indeed be judged "pure" in the terms of another. The formulation of this question as a way of responding to or working with the topic-text may, in a sense, be as playful as is the *iroiro* pun, but if so this is play with a very serious subtext, one that lies not very far beneath its troubled and troubling surface. The poem-speaker's query does not have a clear answer; in the cycle, certainty has been replaced by unease.

Rishubun: The "Understanding the Principle" Chapter [of the *Mahāprajñāpāramitā Sutra*]

(19) [Those who uphold this sutra] shall all be reborn in accordance with their wishes in the various Buddha-lands;

---

46. In the mundane world, lotuses are admired particularly because they grow untainted in muddy waters. In Amida's Pure Land, however, the lotus ponds are fabulously pure, like jewels (*hōchi*).

they shall attain Bodhi and shall never slide back into the evil realms.[47]

izuru hi no ashitagoto ni wa hito shirezu
   nishi ni kokoro wa iru to naranan
Each morning as the sun comes up,
   I wish that my heart might go to the west, and that none
   would know.

Now the poem-speaker reveals something of what is in her heart (*kokoro*): a constantly nurtured desire, but one that must be kept a secret. The particular Buddha-land in which she would wish to be reborn is clearly Amida's (the Pure Land envisioned in the two preceding pairs), which lies in the west, and every morning she prays for such rebirth. There are strong echoes here of Senshi's *omoedomo* poem (as well as of the *Kohon setsuwa shū* account of her habitual daily worship), and here, as in the *omoedomo* poem, the poet reminds herself that no one is supposed to know about her Pure Land-oriented thoughts and prayers—although the poem itself is an admission of them. It is meant, however, to be shared with those who are sure to understand, who surely nurture similar hopes and fears. Like theirs, perhaps, her heart follows the arc of the sun (as does the poem) as it rises in the east (*izuru hi*) and sets in the west (*nishi ni . . . iru*), but her heart does so as if separated from her person, her whole self, which she cannot as yet give entirely to Amida. In the language of love poetry, a lover's heart might be said to go where the body cannot; the yearner may thus achieve an ideal union with the object of its yearning, if not a physical one. The poet's own spiritual journey to the west would also be an extinguishing, like the setting of the sun, yet at the same time would mark the beginning of a new and everlasting life—one from which, as the topic-text promises, she will never fall back into a less perfect state.

Ninnōgyō, first fascicle: The Benevolent Kings Sutra

(20) Conventional truth arises like a phantom,
   Like flowers drifting in a void.[48]

ōzora ni sakitaru hana no fuku kaze ni
   chiru o wagami ni yosoete zo miru

---

47. *T* 7, no. 220, p. 991b.

48. *T* 8, no. 245, p. 829a.

It seems to me that my own self
   is just like these flowers that bloomed and now scatter
   windblown in the sky.

The same, second fascicle

(21) That which exists eventually does not;
   Cause and effect create all things.
   He who flourishes is certain to decline;
   That which is real is actually empty.[49]

hakanaku mo tanomikeru ka na
   hajime yori aru ni mo aranu yo ni koso arikere
It was in vain that I trusted it:
   this is, after all, a life that does not really exist.

The two passages from the *Ninnō hannya haramitsugyō* quoted here and as the topic for the following poem direct the cyclical discourse toward the contemplation of mutability, and that notion is taken up more directly in these poems than in poem 5, which responded rather differently to its topic-text—the most familiar formulaic statement of the doctrine of emptiness and impermanence—from a closely related sutra. In the first *Ninnōgyō* passage, the poet finds a simile (marked clearly by the first two characters of the second couplet) for "conventional truth"[50] that allows her in turn to introduce the conventional figuration of falling blossoms as emblems of transience. She translates the passage's image of "flowers drifting in a void" (*kokū ke*) quite literally—and with a graphic echo, too—as "flowers that are [being blown about by the wind] in the sky" (*ōzora [ni sakitaru] hana*) but adds additional details well suited to a *waka* meditation on the scattering of cherry blossoms. Within the context of the cycle, however, this comparison of the scattered blossoms to the transient self takes on added weight; the poem-speaker is able to perceive the similarity between the falling flowers and herself precisely because the truth about existence has been revealed to her through such texts as that with which this straightforward poem is paired.

   The second *Ninnōgyō* text repeats the doctrine enunciated in the *Hannya shingyō* passage, and again the poet selects language from the

49. *T* 8, no. 245, p. 830a.

50. "Conventional truth" is *setai* (*saṃvṛti satya*, also translated as *zokutai* or *sezokutai*), i.e., the conventional perception of reality, as distinct from "absolute truth," *shintai* (*paramārtha satya*), i.e., perception that is based on an understanding of the nonsubstantiality and emptiness of dharmas.

passage and works it together with related language well suited to *waka* discourse to produce a poem that might, in another context, be readable as the expression of a more secular kind of sentiment. The key word she introduces into the poem for this purpose is *yo*, "the world," or one's existence in it, in this context—but understood in love poetry as the sphere within which men and women meet, entwine, and inevitably part. That "world" of love invariably comes to be seen as empty of anything on which lasting trust can rest (*hakanashi*). To trust it (*tanomu*) or the object of one's love is eventually recognized as an error, and what one thought existed—that love relationship—turns out not to exist at all: *aru ni mo aranu yo ni koso arikere*, in which the pattern *aru ni mo aranu* ("existing but not existing") mimics the reflexive negating patterns of the quotation, which make the same point. In the poem these words are read as the poem-speaker's new realization of the truth—a newly sharpened perception again made possible through the encounter with the sutra-text and through comprehension of its meaning.

Hongan Yakushikyō: The Sutra on Bhaiṣajya-guru's Vows

(22) If but once you hear my name, you will be spared from evil illness, and speedily you will attain the highest form of Bodhi.[51]

hitotabi mo kiku ni wa mina zo tamotaruru
  omoiwazurau wagana naredomo
We all shall be rescued by one hearing of this saving name,
  although my name is that of one who suffers.

The poem's "*wagana*," in the final seven, literally translates the sutra-passage's words for Bhaiṣajya-guru's reference to his own name, and clearly distinguishes itself from "*mina*," in the first seven of the poem, which means "his [the Tathāgata Bhaiṣajya-guru's] name" but also suggests "all of us" by its sound. (Hence, "*mina zo tamotaruru*" means "his is a saving name" as well as "we shall all be saved," with the *-ru[ru]* suffix shifting among its meanings—honorific, potential, and passive.) The *kakekotoba* calls attention to itself, but perhaps even more striking is the poet's interpretation of the "evil illness" (*akubyō*) from which Bhaiṣajya-guru promises to save those who call upon him. This Buddha is usually worshiped as one who cures and prevents physical sickness, but "sickness" (*yamai*) can of course also be interpreted as a metaphor for the unenlightened state, the mental and emotional condition of the individual

---

51. See n. 27, above.

who has not yet found the way to salvation. It is to this sort of suffering that the poem-speaker admits, while affirming her faith in the healing Buddha's promise; and perhaps she deliberately avoids the taboo word *yamai* by substituting *omoiwazurau*. It is not her corporal self (*wagami*) that suffers but that perceived identity that can be known as a nameable self (*wagana*), and its suffering (*omoiwazurau*) is not simply physical but spiritual as well: it stands here for the recurring doubts and frustrations of the poem-speaker.

Jumyōkyō: The Sutra of Long Life

(23) "If you perform a[n abbreviated] reading of this scripture every day for the sake of all sentient beings, you need have no fear of early death or of a shortened span of life."[52]

yosobito no tame ni tamoteru nori yue ni
  kazunaranu mi ni hodo wa henuran
Perhaps it is because I have upheld the Dharma for the sake of others
  that I, though scarcely worthy, have lived this long.

The passage selected from *Jumyōkyō*, an esoteric "*dhāraṇī* sutra," also conveys a promise about the efficacy of a form of devotion—in this case, the "abbreviated reading" (*tendoku*) of the *Jumyōkyō* itself. (The speaker in the sutra is the Buddha himself, responding to the Four Celestial Kings' pleas for a remedy for the sufferings of the sentient.) The poem, however, is one that can be read both as a recognition of the efficacy of this promise and as an anxious but deliberate "misreading" of it; thus, one reading fully accepts the message of the topic-text, while the other responds with deep pessimism. The verb *tamots[u]*, here as in the preceding poem, means "to uphold," "to maintain," and in at least one sense the poet can claim to be "upholding" Buddhism through this composition: by reproducing the words of this and other scriptures (*nori*), and offering her interpretations of them, the poet is indeed sharing these teachings with others (*yosobito*), just as the passage prescribes and as was promised in the preface. (The poem's *yosobito no tame ni* corresponds closely to *i issai shujō* in the topic-text.) The poem-speaker understands that her reward for this and other good deeds may be a long life, even for her humble self (*kazunaranu mi ni hodo wa henuran*: "this corporal self of mine, insignificant though it is, lasting for quite some time"). Yet, if we allow for the possibility that the word *nori* here could also stand for the rules of the religion to which her

---

52. *T* 20, no. 1135, p. 578c.

life is publicly devoted, this poem can be read as one quite similar in spirit to that of the "Mitarashigawa tortoise" poem sent to Higashi Sanjō-in:

> *yosobito no tame ni tamoteru nori yue ni*

Since these are teachings that I uphold for the sake of others [who expect me to maintain the purity of the office of Saiin for their benefit],

> *kazunaranu mi ni hodo wa henuran*

it is my fate [since I cannot practice Buddhist devotions fully and freely] to go on and on for many years as one who is not included in Buddhism's blessings.

The ambiguity that makes these two very different readings possible is not an ambiguity of any of its specific lexical elements but of the poem as a whole as a response to its topic-text. As such, it is perhaps one of the poems in the cycle that best reflects the familiar image of the poet as a woman torn between her public and her private selves.

Muryōgikyō: The Sutra of Innumerable Meanings

> (24) Through discipline, concentration, and wisdom the Buddha ended sensation, achieved liberation, and attained his Buddha body; he attained the Three Illuminations, the Six Transcendental Faculties and the Aspects of the Way, and with great compassion, the Ten Powers, and immovable faith he creates the causes that lead sentient beings toward good karma.[53]

---

53. *T* 9, no. 276, p. 385a. The "Three Illuminations" (*sanmyō*) are three kinds of knowledge: knowledge of one's former lives and of the former lives of others, knowledge of future lives, and knowledge of all forms of suffering in the present and of their cure. The "Six Transcendental Faculties" (*rokutsū*) make it possible for Buddhas and bodhisattvas to manifest themselves anywhere and in any form they wish, and to change the forms of others; to see things at great distances; to hear sounds from great distances; to know the thoughts of others; to know about one's former lives and those of others; and to put an end to all forms of suffering. The "[Thirty-seven] Aspects of the Way" ([*sanjūshichi*] *dōbon*) are various virtuous practices and transcendent attainments achieved on the path toward Nirvana. The "Ten Powers" (*jūriki*) enable a Buddha to know right from wrong; to know all karma of the past, present, and future and its effects; to practice and prioritize all forms of meditation; to perceive the varied capacities of individual sentient beings; to judge what each individual thinks; to know their lineage, temperament, and accomplishments; to know the causes and effects of all practices; to know the form of life taken by each sentient being and the karma that has caused it and will cause future changes; to know how each will die and how each will be reborn; and to know how to end all forms of suffering.

kakubakari hito no kokoro ni makasekeru
   hotoke no tane o motomekeru ka na
I, too, have found the seeds of Buddhahood that he sowed
   so generously in the hearts of us all.

With this topic-text and poem pair, the poet begins the treatment of the "three *Lotus* sutras" (*Hokke sanbukyō*)—the *Muryōgikyō*, the *Lotus* itself, and the *Kanfugengyō*—and her encounters with these central works will occupy most of the remainder of the cycle. Yet there is no particular shift in the cyclical discourse at this point, no demarcator of a new or special section in the text. The general relationship between quotations and poems remains what it was up to this point, and there is the same rising and falling of the poem-speaker's confidence in the messages imparted by the sutras and of her anguish over their applicability to herself.

In poem 24 she responds with affirmation, recognizing that she is indeed one among those for whose sake the Buddha has, through his own good practices, created "causes" that will allow others to cultivate good karma for themselves as well. Her interpretation of the "creating of causes that produce good karma" described in the last seven-character line of the quotation prompts the imagery of the sowing of the seeds of Buddhahood (*hotoke no tane*), but it is particularly in the discovery that these seeds lie even within her own heart that the poem-speaker finds something about which to rejoice (*motomekeru ka na*). The reproduction of the passage and the presentation of the poem with it are the best evidence of that discovery.

Hokekyō jo hon ("Introduction")

> (25) "Again I see Buddha-sons
> Who have never slept,
> Going through forests
> In earnest quest of the Buddha's Path."[54]

---

54. *T* 9, no. 262, p. 3b. The translations of all material from the *Lotus Sutra* used herein are quoted from Hurvitz, *Scripture of the Lotus Blossom of the Fine Dharma*; for this passage, see p. 9. Hurvitz's translation is based on Kumārajīva's translation into Chinese, also the standard text for Japanese Buddhism and, of course, the one from which the quotations for *HSWKS* were taken. In a few instances, however, Hurvitz's consideration of Sanskrit texts obscures the relationship between the Chinese texts reproduced in *HSWKS* and the poems paired with them. These differences are explained in the analyses of those passages in which they occur, below. Transcriptions of the titles of the chapters of the *Lotus Sutra* follow the *kana* glosses in Sakamoto Yukio and Iwamoto Yutaka, eds., *Hokekyo* (Iwanami bunko 33–304–1, 2, and 3), 3 vols. (Tokyo: Iwanami Shoten, 1962–67).

nuru yo naku nori o motomeshi hito mo aru o
   yume no uchi nite sugusu mi zo uki
There were those who forsook sleep each night to seek the
   dharma,
   but how sad to be one who only goes on dreaming.

In this verse section of the *Lotus Sutra*'s prefatory chapter, Maitreya describes the many remarkable efforts that have been made to attain the
Buddha's teachings: among them are those of the "Buddha-sons" (*busshi*)
who spent night after night tramping and pacing through forests in
search of the Way. (*Nuru yo naku* and *nori o motomeshi* are very close
renditions of the second and fourth four-character lines of the quotation;
the verb *motom[u]* echoes from poem 24, as *tamots[u]* did between it and
poem 23.) From these ardent seekers the poem-speaker must separate
herself: she is, unfortunately, one of those who seems never to wake. The
topic-text has offered an image of wakefulness against which the poet can
contrast the familiar figure of the unenlightened state as an endless, troubled dream, and the poem's departure from the word and spirit of the
quoted passage parallels the poet's sense of distance from her goals. The
waka is as different and distanced from the passage to which it responds
as the poet is different and distanced from her ideal.

   Hōben bon ("Expedient Devices")

   (26) "If anyone, even with distracted thought,
         And with so much as a single flower,
         Makes offering to a painted image,
         He shall at length see numberless Buddhas."[55]

hitotabi no hana no kaori o shirube nite
   musu no hotoke ni aimizarameya
With the scent of just one flower as my guide,
   won't I, too, see all the numberless Buddhas?

While the topic-text—part of a verse-passage in which the Buddha explains a number of methods of worship (*hōben*) and their results to
Śāriputra—describes a direct cause and effect, the poem, by figuring the
scent of the flower as a *shirube* ("guide"), begins to suggest a visionary
journey: the worshiper, guided by the offered flower, can expect to move
into the world envisioned by the painting and see the myriad Buddhas it

---

55. *T* 9, p. 9a; Hurvitz, *Scripture of the Lotus Blossom*, 40.

depicts in full dimension. The word *shirube* here is reminiscent of its appearances in poems where the scent of flowers guides warblers into the open, or a helpful wind guides a small boat into open waters,[56] but it transfers easily to the context of spiritual guidance.[57] The poet does not use the notion of a "distracted mind" (*sanranshin*) to refer overtly to her own troubled state: to do so would in fact be a misreading, since the phrase indicates that the offering of the flower will have its effect even when it is offered casually, with little serious thought about the results to be gained thereby. But perhaps there is some sense of the poem-speaker's own uncertainty about her capacities behind her nonetheless hopeful rhetorical question, "Will I not see them before my own eyes, too (*aimizarameya*)?"

Hiyu hon ("Parables")

(27) "Goat-drawn carriages, deer drawn carriages,
And carriages drawn by great oxen

---

56. See *Kokin wakashū* no. 13 (Ki no Tomonori):

> *hana no ka o kaze no tayori ni taguete zo*
> *uguisu sasou shirube ni wa yaru*
> Let me send the scent of these blossoms with a letter in the wind,
> to guide the warbler to come near.

and no. 472 (Fujiwara no Kachion):

> *shiranami no ato naki kata ni yuku fune mo*
> *kaze zo tayori no shirube narikeru*
> The wind, at least, is a helpful guide
> for the departing boat that leaves no traces in the white waves.

(*SKT* 1, 10, 20.) As in the *HSWKS* poem, the *shirube* in the latter poem guides the eye of the viewer (the poem-speaker) toward a yearned-for object.

57. In *Genji monogatari,* when Hikaru Genji hears voices at prayer near the house where he has spent the night with Yūgao, he murmurs a poem:

> *ubasoku ga okonau michi o shirube nite*
> *kon yo mo fukaki chigiri tagau na*
> With the rites the adept performs as our guide,
> what can keep us from the meeting we now so fervently promise to have
> in the world beyond?

In the "*Yūgao*" chapter; see Abe Akio, Akiyama Ken, and Imai Gen'ei, eds., *Genji monogatari* 1 (*Nihon koten bungaku zenshū* 12) (Tokyo: Shōgakukan, 1980), 232. The aura of the *ubasoku* as spiritual guide is manipulated here in a seemingly passionate but, in the context, suitably creepy love poem.

Now outside the door
Come out, all of you!"[58]

amata ari to kado o ba kikite ideshikado
   hitotsu no nori no kuruma narikeri
They heard, "There are many," and rushed outdoors to see—
   but they found, after all, that there was only one carriage
   to ride in, one vehicle of the dharma.

The quoted excerpt from the *gātha* retelling of the "Parable of the Burning House" provides the poet with an opportunity to return to the play with the word *nori* that involves its meanings as both "riding on a vehicle" and "dharma"; the passage is, in fact, a kind of locus classicus for the figuration that is part of what makes such wordplay possible. The speaker of the quoted lines is a father, owner of the "Burning House," pleading with his children to detach themselves from their amusements inside—lest they perish in the flames—and turn to the attractions of the "carriages" (*sha*, a kind of "*norimono*") that he has provided in order to carry them away from destruction. (The father's words are quoted by the Buddha as he tells the parable.) In the parable, of course, the burning house stands for the world of attachment that produces suffering, and each of the "carriages" is a vehicle (*yāna*), an interpretation of Buddhist teachings that can convey attached and suffering beings away from that world. The poem reiterates the point of the parable, and one of the major points of the sutra: that the many "vehicles" are really only one, provided by the Buddha (like the father) to save his "children." But the poem can be read either as a report of the interplay between the father and his children that illustrates this, or, substituting "I" for "they" in the translation, as the poem-speaker's re-enactment of their experience: *hitotsu no nori no kuruma narikeri*, thus, may mean "it turned out to be just one vehicle of the dharma" or "I realized then that it was just one [when I read the passage reproduced here]."

Shinge hon ("Belief and Understanding")

(28) "He showed him his gold and silver,
   His pearls and *sphāṭika*,
   The income and expenditure of his various things
   Making him responsible for them all.
   Yet the son still lived outside the gate,
   Dwelling in a grass hut . . ."[59]

---

58. *T* 9, p. 14b; Hurvitz, *Scripture of the Lotus Blossom*, 69.

59. *T* 9, p. 18a; Hurvitz, ibid., 93–94.

> *kusa no io ni toshiheshi hodo no kokoro ni wa*
>   *tsuyu kakaran to omoigakekiya*
> Among his thoughts through the years passed in that grass
>   hut,
>   did he ever have an inkling of the blessings that would fall
>   on him?

The passage comes from the versified reiteration of the parable that domi-
nates this chapter, a story of a rich man and his son. The son, having
returned home after many years of beggarly life, spends yet another
twenty years working as his father's servant and living in humble quarters
outside his father's mansion, unaware of his rightful place, until he gradu-
ally acquires the capacity to inherit the family's wealth and is enlightened
as to his true status by his father. The Buddha's disciples use the parable to
praise the Buddha for having withheld his ultimate teaching—the *Lotus*
itself—until they were ready for it. The "grass hut" (*sōan*) in which the son
lived for so long appears in the poem (*kusa no io*) and prompts the introduction of *tsuyu*, "dew," conventionally associated with the "grass hut"
because dew rests on grass (*kusa . . . ni . . . tsuyu kakar[u]*) but usually
suggestive of the tears shed by the lonely hermit who dwells therein.[60]
Here, however, the coming of the dew to the grass hut refers to the new
knowledge and great riches that befall the son when he is ready to accept
them: simultaneously, *tsuyu* functions idiomatically with *omoigak[u]* to
ask, "Did he have *even the least idea* of what was to come?" The poem
focuses on the dramatic irony of the parable: "The son knew nothing of
what awaited him, did he? But how rich were his ultimate rewards!"
Again, the language of the poem is sufficiently ambiguous to allow for an
alternately personalized reading: "Through all the years that I dwelt here
in these conditions, has it ever occurred to me that such blessings could
be mine?"

Yakusōyu hon ("Medicinal Herbs")

(29) "[. . . this dharma is]
    To be likened to a great cloud,
    Which with the rain of a single flavor
    Moistens human flowers
    Enabling each to perfect its fruit."[61]

---

60. Katagiri Yōichi, *Utamakura utakotoba jiten*, 136.

61. *T* 9, p. 20b; Hurvitz, *Scripture of the Lotus Blossom*, 109. The bracketed text is not part of
    the quotation used by the poet, which begins *in medias res* with "it is, for example, like
    a great cloud . . ." without indicating that it is "the dharma preached by the Buddha"
    that is being described by this analogy.

hitotsu iro ni wagami utsuredo hana no iro mo
  nishi ni sasu e ya nioimasuran[62]
I appear to have the same color as others do,
    but don't the flowers on the branch that catches the light
    from the west have the richer hue?

In the *Yakusōyu* chapter of the *Lotus,* the Buddha explains to Kāśyapa that different people receive his single teaching in different ways: the teaching is likened to sweet rain that has but a single flavor (*ichimi no ame*), yet causes the many kinds of plants upon which it falls to grow and flourish in their diverse ways. The analogy to humans is made almost too explicit by the word "human flowers" (*ninge*) in the third four-character line of the quotation from the versified reiteration of this discourse. But this imagery in the sutra is very well suited to the traditional imagery of *waka,* and the poet knows how to deploy it. At the same time, however, she again asks a question suggestive of anxiety over her own exclusion from the Buddha's blessings. Speaking as the flower (*hana*) and/or for herself (*wagami*) figured as the flower, she observes that she, like all her equals, is "imbued with the same color" (*hitotsu iro ni . . . utsuredo,* where *iro* replaces *mi/aji* and *utsur[u],* "take on a color," replaces *jun/uruos[u],* "moisten," as the poet interprets and recasts the imagery)—in other words, their essential nature is the same. Yet, she asks, are not the flowers that bloom on branches that bask in the light that comes from the west—the light that shines from the direction of Amida's Pure Land—still deeper of color as well as stronger of scent? (*Nio[u]* can mean both.) In other words, are not those who can turn full face to the west and openly express their devotion more truly blessed than those who cannot? Though the topic-text's context is a recapitulation of the idea that the Buddha adjusts his teachings and his ways of giving them according to the capacities of each recipient, this poem-speaker remains painfully conscious of the special limitations that make her "different." She is as ill at ease, and for the same reasons, as is the speaker of Senshi's "*omoedomo*" poem as she turns her face in secrecy toward the western light.

Juki hon ("Bestowal of Prophecy")

(30) "If, knowing our deepest thoughts
    And perceiving that we are the recipients of this
      prophecy,

---

62. The Shoryōbu texts both read ". . . *nishi ni sasu hi ya nioimasuran* 西にさす ひや匂ひますらん," judged a mistranscription by both Ishihara and Hashimoto.

He sprinkles sweet dew on us,
He will thereby rid us of oppressive heat, and we
shall be cool."[63]

nori omou kokoro shi fukaku narinureba
tsuyu no sora ni mo suzushikarikeri
Since their hearts yearned intensely for the dharma
they were cooled by the dew that filled the air.

The speakers of the verse in the scripture are the disciples
Maudgalyāyana, Subhūti, and Mahākātyāyana, and they are pleading
with the Buddha to give each of them a prophecy of their future Buddhahood, as he has just done for their fellow disciple Kāśyapa. He does
so, and poem 30 affirms this while accommodating the resonant metaphor
of "cooling dew." *Nori omou kokoro shi fukaku nar[u]* ("The heart[s] that
yearn[ed] for the dharma were deep[ly sincere]") is also a variation on
elements in the first line of the quoted passage (. . . *waga shinjin* . . .); in
the poem, the "sincere heart" is posited as a condition that produced a
result, the "cooling" of the heat that oppressed the supplicants. (The
presence here of the cooling "sweet dew" [*kanro/tsuyu*] also links this
topic-text and poem pair to the watery imagery of that which precedes it.
These are good examples of passages that are in a sense representative of
the chapters from which they are taken, but that appear to have been
chosen precisely because they offered appropriate and useful imagery.)
The final five, *suzushikarikeri*, may literally translate the quotation's "they
attained coolness," but its *-keri* ending is again one of the things that
makes it possible to read this poem as one voiced by a stronger individual
identity: "My heart was sincere in its longing for the dharma, and so I
have been cooled by the dews that fill the air." In this case, it would seem,
the anxieties of the poem-speaker have at least temporarily been assuaged
by this encounter with the scripture.

Kejōyu hon ("Parable of the Conjured City")

(31) Throughout the long night of time they gain in
        evil destinies
     And reduce the ranks of the gods.
     From darkness proceeding to darkness,
     They never hear the Buddha's name.[64]

---

63. *T* 9, p. 21a; Hurvitz, *Scripture of the Lotus Blossom*, 122.

64. *T* 9, p. 22c; Hurvitz, ibid., 133.

kuraki yori kuraki ni nagaku irinutomo
tazunete tare ni towan to suran
From darkness into darkness, on and on I'll plunge—
but whom can I turn to to show me the way?

As we have seen, this passage was well established as a poem-topic, and it is hard to imagine that the poet was unaware of its potency, or of Izumi Shikibu's poem that exercises it. (See the discussion in part 1.) Both poets crafted their first three lines (5–7–5) as virtually intact translations of the third line of the original passage (as it is quoted here). *Nagaku*, interpolated into the first seven-syllable section in the present poem, is brought there from the fourth phrase in the quotation, where it describes the length of time that ignorant sufferers must spend without the transforming experience of "hearing the Buddha's name"; in the poem, however, it indicates the length of the poem-speaker's journey into darkness. The character for "hear" in "hear the Buddha's name" can mean "inquire" as well, and it is this nuance that is developed in *tazunete* tare ni *towan* to suran ("should I *inquire* for guidance, of whom shall I *ask* it?"). The poem-speaker does not seem at all sure that guidance will be forthcoming; she expects, rather, to journey still further into a dark landscape where no sun, moon, or any other source of light will shine.

Gohyaku deshi juki hon ("Receipt of Prophecy by Five Hundred Disciples")

(32) "Taking a priceless jewel,
[The rich man] attaches it to his friend's garment
inside,
Then, leaving it in silence, he goes away,
While his friend, lying down at the time, is aware of
nothing."[65]

ei no uchi ni kakeshi koromo no tamatama mo
mukashi no tomo ni aite koso shire
All these jewels, sewn into my robes while I was drunk—
I discovered them only when I chanced to meet my old
friend again.

The "Parable of the Jewel in the Robe"—the story of a man who endured great poverty unaware that a wealthy friend had long ago sewn precious

---

65. *T* 9, p. 29b; Hurvitz, ibid., 166.

jewels into the garment he has managed to keep with him through his
travails—also served frequently as a poem-topic on occasions when compositions about the *Lotus* or passages in it were called for.[66] Aside from its
potent message about the presence of the inherent Buddha-nature in all
persons, it could be turned into a parable of the discovery of the *Lotus*
itself, the trope of the "drunken stupor" (*ei*) replacing "endless dream" or
"endless night" as the prelude to awakening and the discovery of the
jewel.[67] Moreover, the focal elements of the parable—the robe (*koromo*)
and the jewel (*tama*)—were readily accommodated to *waka* contexts. In
secular *waka* the phrase *koromo no tama* was used frequently as a trope for
"tears,"[68] but in this poem, *tama*, in *koromo no tama*, is "the jewel in the
robe," and also part of "*tamatama*," an adverbial, "by chance, just now."
The poem-speaker also speaks simultaneously in two ways, as the man
who finds the treasure he has so long but so unwittingly possessed when
he is once again in the company of his "old friend" (*mukashi no tomo*) and
as another identity, who, having encountered (or reencountered) this
instructive parable in the text—another sort of "old friend," a revered
scripture handed down lovingly through time—has indeed learned something new from it.

> *Jugaku-mugakuninki hon* ("Prophecies Conferred on
> Learners and Adepts")

> (33) "O World-Honored one! O Lamp of Wisdom!
>   Since we have heard the sound of prophecy,
>   Our hearts are full of joy,
>   As if we had been infused with sweet dew."[69]

---

66. See, for example, *Akazome Emon shū* no. 8, a poem that (according to the *kotobagaki*)
    played a role in a flirtatious exchange with a man attending a "Service of Eight
    Lectures on the *Lotus*" (*hakkō*). On the other hand, poem 434 in the same collection—
    Akazome Emon's *Gohyaku [deshi juki] hon* poem in her *nijūhappon no uta* series—is
    much more straightforward (*SKT* 3, 312, 322). See also Kintō's poem for his series,
    Kintō shū no. 266 (ibid., 305), and, for slightly later examples, *Jōjin ajari no haha shū*
    nos. 83 and 99 (ibid., 374–75).

67. The familiarity of the trope is suggested by its use in the preface to the second volume
    of tales in *Sanbōe*; see Koizumi and Takahashi, *Shohon taishō Sanbōe shūsei*, 90; and
    Kamens, *The Three Jewels*, 165.

68. *Goshūi wakashū* nos. 1027 and 1028 display an interesting exercise of these conven-
    tional elements, in which tears are shed over a robe that until recently belonged to a
    certain gentleman who has become a monk. See *SKT* 1, 134.

69. *T* 9, p. 30b; Hurvitz, *Scripture of the Lotus Blossom*, 173.

akirakeki nori no tomoshibi nakariseba
  kokoro no yami no ikade haremashi
Were there not this brilliant torchlight of the dharma,
  how could this darkness be driven from my heart?

Hosshi hon ("Preachers of Dharma")

(34) "[If a man is] lonely, without a human sound,
    There reading or reciting this scriptural canon,
    At that time I will appear to him, displaying
    A body of pure radiance."[70]

sora sumite kokoro nodokeki sayonaka ni
  ariake no tsuki no hikari o zo masu
At midnight, the sky is clear, my heart is calm,
  and the light of the moon at dawn will grow still brighter.

Ken hōtō hon ("Apparition of the Jeweled Stupa")

(35) "Thereupon with his right finger Śākyamunibuddha
opened the door of the seven-jeweled stūpa, which made a
great sound . . ."[71]

tama no to o hirakishi toki ni awazu shite
  akenu yo ni shi mo madoubeshi ya wa
Absent when he opened the jeweled door,
  must I lose my way in this unending night?

The *gātha* that serves as the topic for poem 33 is uttered in ecstasy by two
thousand "learners and those who had nothing more to learn" who have
all received predictions of their future Buddhahood.[72] The poet selects the
figure of the Buddha as a bright torchlight (*etōmyō*) as the dominant image
of her poem, too—but sets aside the "sweet dew" (*kanro*) and its potential
nuances. Her "torch" (*tomoshibi*) is in fact not the Buddha whose praises
are sung in the *gātha* with this figure: it is, instead, his illuminating teachings (*akirakeki nori no tomoshibi*), and where the ecstatic recipients of prophecy sing of the joy that fills their hearts, the poem-speaker acknowledges—by asking a question with an obvious answer (in a very familiar

---

70. *T* 9, p. 32b; Hurvitz, ibid., 182.

71. *T* 9, p. 33b; Hurvitz, ibid., 187.

72. Ibid.

rhetorical pattern[73])—that it is the dharma torch that has or surely will drive away the darkness that is in her own heart (*kokoro no yami*). *Kokoro no yami* is an image that often appears in poems about a parent's anxieties for a child or lovers driven to distraction by frustrated yearning.[74] Here it is brought into play with the imagery of the torch not only to create a variation on the *gātha* but also to add to the cycle yet another poem that describes a spiritual darkness into which bright light has been or will be cast.[75] The following poems sustain this theme.

The extraction from their larger context of the four lines of five characters that constitute the topic-text for poem 34 leaves a jagged edge; the preceding two lines (in Hurvitz' translation: "If a man preaching Dharma/ is alone in a quiet and idle place . . .") make it clear that it is a person, a devotee of this scripture, who is pictured, and the whole passage is the Buddha's promise to appear in visible form as a companion to such a person when he finds himself in isolation, as a sign of that person's great spiritual achievement. The *waka* response paints an even more evocative scene of profound quiet and of expectation. While it places the poem-speaker in conditions like those posited for the lonely "preacher of dharma," and appropriates his expectations, it does so in language that might well serve as that of a contemplative poet, man or woman, who has

73. Narihira's "*yo no naka ni taete sakura no nakariseba* . . .," discussed above, is a prototype. See part one, n. 29. Also compare *Akazome Emon shū* poem 531 (*SKT* 3, 324):

> yo o terasu nori no tomoshibi nakariseba
> hotoke no michi o ikade shiramashi
> Were there not this torchlight of the dharma shining in the world,
>   how would we find our way to the Buddha Path?

74. A poem by Fujiwara Kanesuke—*Gosen wakashū* no. 1102 (*SKT* 1, 56), also in *Yamato monogatari* section 45—may well be the template for such imagery: it is frequently imitated and alluded to in other works, particularly in *Genji monogatari*. See also *Ise monogatari* section 69. When Senshi received a request from her elder sister Shishi Naishinnō for something written in the hand of their late father Murakami, she sent along a poem (so the *kotobagaki* in *Gyokuyō wakashū* tells us) with this twist of the familiar *kokoro no yami* motif:

> ko o omou michi koso yami to kikishikado
> oya no ato ni mo mayowarenikeri
> I have heard it said that the path of the loving parent is a dark one, yet now it
>   is I who am lost, left behind here among my father's traces.

(*Gyokuyō wakashū* no. 2420; *SKT* 1, 472.)

75. Compare *Senzai wakashū* no. 1242, a *daiei* composition on "the *kokoro* of" a passage in the [*Nyorai*] *Jinriki bon* of the *Lotus Sutra* ("[As] the bright lights of the sun and moon completely disperse the darkness") by "Priest Renjō":

sat through the night, serene yet full of anticipation, watching the sky and the moon for meaningful portents. (As we have seen, the two collections of Saiin poems suggest that Senshi and her attendants spent many such wakeful nights, tracking the course of the moon through the sky, composing poems on what they saw and what it seemed to signify.) The poem-speaker's mind is as clear and tranquil as the sky that arches above her: *kokoro* reflects *sora*, and vice versa. But when the midnight sky yields to the dawn, an ever-brightening light shed by the moon, appearing, as does the radiant Buddha, to dispel the lingering darkness, will shine into this tranquility, transforming it to another and still greater peace. The poem-speaker has calmed herself and is prepared to wait for the sign that heralds that great peace: she knows that she will see it.

The topic-text for poem 35 omits the simile that follows in this prose-passage of the sutra: "as of a bar being pushed aside to open the gate of a walled city."[76] But the poet takes up the imagery of the "opening door" and does two striking things with it that are characteristic of her method throughout the cycle. First, she plays on the relationship between *hirak[u]*, "open" (the character for which, *kai*, is present in the second group of four characters in the quoted prose) and *ak[u]*, also "open," as of a door but also, as it is used and written in the poem, as in "the opening of day"— the brightening of the night sky as dawn approaches. (As used in the poem, *hirak[u]* is a transitive verb, *ak[u]* is intransitive: thus, "he opened the door" is juxtaposed with "the night that does not brighten." In all of the *Hosshin wakashū* copies *tama no to* is written "the jeweled *door*," but the sound of this also suggests "the jeweled *stupa* [*tō*]).

Second, with a forcefulness that demands as much attention as does her wordplay, the poem-speaker makes herself present in the moment of the poem's delivery. She does so through her rhetorical question, *madoubeshi ya wa*, asked of the topic-text as well as of the reader as interlocutor. Yet at the same time she refers to her absence (*awazu shite*, "as I did not encounter/was not present at that scene") from the spectacular moment described in the quotation. "*Akenu yo*," the night to which no dawn comes, in which the poem-speaker emphatically situates herself, also recapitulates the previous topic-text and poem pair's imagery of dark

---

hi no hikari tsuki no kage to zo terashikeru
kuraki kokoro no yami hareyo to te
Like the rays of the sun, the brightness of the moon, it shines as if to say
"Confusion, begone from all hearts that now are dark."

(SKT 1, 214; Ishihara, *Shakkyōka no kenkyū*, 269.)

76. *T* 9, p. 33b; Hurvitz, *Scripture of the Lotus Blossom*, 187.

and light. But no dawn moon sheds its light here. Indeed, the poem-
speaker wonders whether or not her endless night can be brought to an
end if she cannot be as true a witness to the verity of the Buddha's
teachings as were the multitudes who did see the "opening" of the jeweled stupa in all its brilliance. And what answer does the poem-speaker
expect? Is it, "Yes, since you are so distanced from such times, places, and
conditions, you must continue to endure your suffering," or, "No, it does
not matter that you 'were not there ; your darkness, too, can and will be
replaced by light"? Either would fit one of her shifts between pessimistic
doubt and confident hope, the interplay of which is as mutable as that of
the light and dark that symbolize them.

> *Daibadatta hon* ("Devadatta")

> (36) ". . . all from a distance seeing that dragon girl
> achieve Buddhahood and universally preach Dharma to the
> men and gods of the assembly of that time were overjoyed at
> heart . . ."[77]

> *sawari ni mo sawaranu tameshi arikereba*
> *hedatsuru kumo mo araji to zo omou*
> Here is the example of one who was not obstructed by the
>   Obstructions,
>   so I, too, can hope that no more clouds will block my way.

The response to this prose-passage that describes another spectacular
moment in the *Lotus* narrative—that moment when the daughter of the
dragon king, having instantaneously changed gender, is revealed and
hailed as a great Buddha—is more positive than that expressed in the
preceding *waka*. This poem is structured around words that have to do
with obstruction, *sawar[u]* and *hedats[u]*, present here as overtones from
the context of the quoted passage—the dragon girl's overcoming of the
unique obstacles that bar women from Buddhahood—rather than as repe-
titions or reconstructions of the language of the passage itself. (*Sawari ni
mo sawaranu* also recapitulates the circular negation encountered in poem
21 [*aru ni mo aranu*].) In the sutra the multitudes who witness the transformation of the girl into a Buddha enthroned in glory see that Buddha far

---

77. *T* 9, p. 35c; Hurvitz, ibid., 201. The Nāga girl episode is preceded in the chapter by the
    account of the long-ago Buddha-to-be's years of service with an ascetic, later reborn as
    Devadatta. As noted above, the ascetic episode was also of great interest to lay
    devotees of the *Lotus*, and not infrequently the topic of poems. Like Senshi, Akazome
    Emon addresses the Nāga girl topic at this same point in her *nijūhappon no uta* series
    (*SKT* 3, 242), but Kintō's has two poems, one on each episode (ibid., 305).

above them in the sky, and this positioning may be part of what prompts the poet to describe "clouds" as the kind of obstacle that, she is now willing to believe, need not necessarily stand between her and her goals. Such interfering clouds (*hedatsuru kumo*) in *waka* stand between the humble and the mighty, the living and the dead, one lover and another, as well as between the spiritually yearning and the spiritually fulfilled. Here, they may also represent the protective and hence limiting aura that surrounds the poet in the ritual role she is compelled to play, even while she yearns to proceed toward another sort of life. But there is hope, the poem-speaker seems to say, that even this obstruction can be dispelled. "*Araji to zo omou*"—"I do believe that these clouds shall be gone"—comes as close to all-but-complete confidence as does any language in the cycle.

Kanji hon ("Fortitude")

(37) ". . . to preach this scripture,
       [We] will endure these troubles.
       We do not covet bodily life,
       We do but regret the Unexcelled Path."[78]

ukikoto no shinobigataki o shinobitemo
   nao kono michi o oshimi todomen
Though I shall endure sorrows that are beyond endurance,
   I shall remain, resolute, in this Path.

Anrakugyō hon ("Comfortable Conduct")

(38) "If in a quiet place
       One perfects and collects one's thoughts,
       Dwelling securely and unmoving
       As if one were Mt. Sumeru itself . . ."[79]

sadamenaki yo mo nani narazu
   nori o omou kokoro no uchi shi ugoki nakereba
This fickle world means nothing to me, for in this heart,
   wherein I contemplate the dharma, there is no change.

---

78. *T* 9, p. 36c; Hurvitz, *Scripture of the Lotus Blossom*, 206.

79. *T* 9, p. 37c; Hurvitz, ibid., 212.

Jūjiyujutsu bon ("Welling Up Out of the Earth")

(39) "They have well learned the bodhisattva-path, and
They are untainted by worldly dharmas,
Like the lotus blossom in the water.
Out of earth welling up . . ."[80]

isagiyoki hito no michi ni mo irinureba
mutsu no chiri ni mo kegarezarikeri
Since I have set out upon the path of those who are pure,
I shall no longer be sullied by the Six Dusts.

Three poems of firm resolve follow one upon the other at this point in the cycle, perhaps as an expansion upon the optimism voiced in no. 36. The quotation from the *Kanji hon*—two couplets of a *gātha*, in five-character lines—is part of an avowal, uttered by a vast chorus of bodhisattvas, of determination to uphold the *Lotus,* to preach it and spread its teachings even in the face of ridicule, censure, and physical torture. The grammatical subject of the poem could be their "we" (*gatō/warera* are the first characters in the couplet preceding the quotation and *ga* is the first character of the second couplet in it), but it can also be the "I" of the singular poem-speaker who echoes their resolve. The verbs *shinob[u]* (endure) and *oshim[u]* (translated by Hurvitz as "regret," perhaps better as "have a care about," "wish to protect") come directly from the quotation, reinforcing the echo effect. The circularity of *shinobigataki o shinobitemo* may also echo *sawari ni mo sawaranu* in poem 36. The structures are grammatically different, but both convey the idea of cancellation: the obstructions do not obstruct; the unbearable nevertheless is borne. The poet's perseverance may not cause her the kinds of physical suffering that the *gātha*-speakers enumerate, but the "sorrows" (*ukikoto,* corresponding to the quotation's *shonanji*) are a comparable price to pay for the prize she seeks, and a price she is willing to accept.

The speaker of the *Anrakugyō hon* quotation—two couplets of four characters each—is Śākyamuni Buddha, advising Mañjuśrī on the cultivation of tranquility and steadiness, qualities as essential for attaining Buddhahood and keeping the *Lotus* as the fierce determination proclaimed in

---

80. *T* 9, p. 42a; Hurvitz, ibid., 235. Hurvitz treats "out of earth welling up" as the first part of a "sentence" within the *gātha* that continues, "They all produce the thought of humble veneration,/Remaining in the presence of the World-Honored One." In the Chinese, "out of earth welling up" can be read as part of the description of the emergence of thousands of bodhisattvas who spring out of the earth just as lotuses rise from beneath the water's surface.

the preceding chapter. The poem contrasts the mutable mundane (*sadamenaki yo*), so unworthy of notice (*nani narazu*), with "movement" (*ugoki*) away from the heart's goal, now an impossibility precisely because the "world" is understood to be so unreliable.[81] The poem-speaker may speak in general about the steadfast heart that cannot be distracted from its true goal; *nori o omou* may mean "keep the dharma in mind" or "yearn for the dharma." But the poem may also be her own proclamation that "I shall not be moved." The language of fixedness figured in the topic-text by the mass of Mt. Sumeru is transferred to the poem's subject: *fudō* is literally reread as *ugoki na[shi]*, but its focus has shifted from the person pictured in the topic-text to the person in the poem.

Maitreya is the speaker of the lines quoted from the *Jūjiyujutsu hon*, and in this *gātha* he praises the virtues of the myriad bodhisattvas who have sprung up out of the earth itself to spread the *Lotus* teachings eternally among the sentient. Again, substituting "they" for "I," one can read the poem as a description of those bodhisattvas, echoing Maitreya's praise. But the poem-speaker can also be suggesting that because she has resolved to emulate them (and is in a sense doing so by composing this cycle), she has indeed entered the path of the pure. By setting out on that path, she has made herself comparable to them in cleanliness (a cleanliness different from that produced by her Kamo lustrations) and has set herself apart from the rest of the world, which can no longer taint her. The "Six Dusts" (*rokujin/mutsu no chiri*[82]) are not mentioned in the quotation, nor in the *gātha* of which it is a part: the term is introduced here as an interpretation of "tainting worldly dharmas" (*sekenbō*), as counterpoint to the language of purity (*isagiyoshi, kegarezarikeri*), and to stand for all the deceptive attractions of mundane life on which the poem-speaker says she has turned her back forever. The diametric opposition of the pure path and the sullied world is further emphasized by syntactic parallelism: *isagiyoki hito no michi ni mo* ("even" or "at least in the path of the pure"), *mutsu no chiri no naka ni mo* ("even amidst the Six Dusts").

---

81. The phrase "*sadamenaki yo*"—a world (or worldly existence) that is constantly shifting, indeterminate, inscrutable—is *kago*, poetic diction, with a strong pedigree established, for example, in *Gosen wakashū* no. 1344 and *Shūi wakashū* no. 734 (*SKT* 1, 63, 80). See also its use in two of the poems of a set composed on a misty summer morning at the Saiin (*Daisaiin saki no gyoshū* nos. 196 and 198). "*Sadamenaki*" may also describe churning waves (*nami*), shifting breezes (*kaze*), fickle hearts (*kokoro*), and the uncertain and unreliable self (*mi*).

82. The "Six Dusts" are the six objects of the sense organs (*rokkon*—eyes, ears, nose, tongue, body, and mind), i.e., color and form, sound, odor, taste, that which can be touched, and that which the mind fixes itself upon.

Nyorai juryō hon ("The Life-span of the Thus Come One")

(40) "For the beings' sake,
      And as an expedient device, I make a show of
        nirvāṇa,
      Yet in fact I do not pass into extinction,
      But ever dwell here and preach Dharma.
      I, ever dwelling here,
      By the power of my supernatural penetrations,
      Cause the topsy-turvy living beings,
      Though they are near, not to see."[83]

sono kami no kokoromadoi no nagori nite
chikaki o minu zo wabishikarikeru
As a lingering effect of the confusion that was in my heart
I failed, alas, to see what was so close at hand.

In the seventh parable of the *Lotus*, a major feature of this chapter, the
Buddha tells about a great physician who returns from a journey to find
his many sons so ill from imbibing medicines other than his own that they
are nearly insane (their minds are "topsy-turvy," *tentō*, driven into error).
Some of them accept his good medicine and are cured; others refuse—too
crazed to recognize the good medicine as such, and only awaken to its
virtues and are thereby cured after their father's death. The Buddha thus
explains that some beings know him here and now, while others must
wait until long after he has passed into extinction (or appears to have done
so) before they can accept his teachings. The poem in response to the
lines quoted from the *gātha* that reiterates the parable translates the
"topsy-turvy" state of the sick and misguided as *kokoromadoi*, a confusion
in the mind and heart that is akin to the "darkness of the heart" (*kokoro no
yami*) of poem 33. *Chikaki o minu*, "not seeing that which is close," translates the language of the last line of the quotation even more literally. The
poem-speaker perceives in retrospect that she has been the victim of
blinding mental and emotional distraction analogous to the drug-induced
madness of the physician's sons. Diagnosis of the cause of the poem-
speaker's daze is left to the reader's interpretation. It may simply be a
question of disposition, as the parable suggests, or it may be the conse-
quence of living a life divided by inimical interests. But such confusion
can be consigned to the past (*sono kami*): now the poem-speaker is fully
prepared to embrace that which has always been so near yet just beyond
her reach.

---

83. *T* 9, p. 43b; Hurvitz, *Scripture of the Lotus Blossom*, 242.

Funbetsu kudoku hon ("Discrimination of Merits")

(41) "There rain down heavenly *māndārava*s
And *mahāmāndārava*s
And *Śakra*s and *Brahmā*s, like Ganges' sands
In their numberlessness, come from the Buddha-
lands.
Candana and incense that sinks in water rain down
In a jumble, falling in confusion
Like birds flying down from the sky,
Scattered as offerings over the Buddhas."[84]

iroiro no hana chirikureba
kumoi yori tobikau tori to miemagaiken
When so many flowers of so many kinds fell all around me,
I took them to be soaring birds whose many paths were
crossing in the sky.

Zuiki kudoku hon ("The Merits of Appropriate Joy")

(42) "The world is in no wise firm or secure,
But it is like water-bubbles, like a will-o'-the-wisp!
You all must
Speedily produce thoughts of revulsion!"[85]

kagerō no aru ka naki ka no yo no naka ni
ware aru mono to tare tanomiken
In this will-o'-the-wisp world that exists and then does not,
who could have had faith in her own existence?

Hosshi kudoku hon ("The Merits of the Dharma-Preacher")

(43) "Also, as in a pure, bright mirror
One sees all physical images,
The bodhisattva, in his pure body,
Sees whatever is in the world."[86]

---

84. *T* 9, p. 44c; Hurvitz, ibid., 248.

85. *T* 9, p. 47b; Hurvitz, ibid., 261.

86. *T* 9, p. 50a; Hurvitz, ibid., 275.

kumori naki kagami no uchi zo hazukashiki
kagami no kage no kumori nakereba
The image in the mirror that reflects so perfectly fills me with
shame,
for nothing clouds the reflection in it.

The seventeenth, eighteenth, and nineteenth chapters of the *Lotus* form a group within the sutra: each explicates the rewards that come to those who preach, promote, and protect the sutra itself. But the quotations used as themes here are not particularly pertinent to these themes; rather, as we have seen elsewhere, they appear to have been selected primarily because they contain images and figural language that could effectively be worked into *waka*. In the *gāthā* from which the topic-lines for poem 41 are taken, Maitreya is describing the miraculous effects that accompany the Buddha's preaching of the scripture, and among these is a rain of celestial flowers (*māndārava* and *mahāmāndārava*) and of incense that is showered upon the many Buddhas who come to hear and bear witness to the teaching. The simile "like birds flying down from the sky" in the *gāthā* actually describes the rain of incense, but the poet transfers it to the falling of the flowers, and the poem-speaker (the person to whom the flowers looked like and were mistaken for birds [. . . *tori to miemagaiken*]) describes her experience of a visual and poetic confusion like that of those who witness the Buddha's preaching. It is, moreover, a confusion like that of the many other poem-speakers who have mistaken scattering snow for blossoms, or, conversely, blossoms for snow.[87] Thus, besides reenacting a familiar poetic pose (thereby making the poem most obviously like other *waka*), the poet appropriates the vision seen in the sutra and reproduces it in the present of the poetic utterance.

The two couplets quoted from the *Zuiki kudoku hon* are words that the Buddha says a "great donor" (*daiseshu*) should preach to the multitudes he has supported through life as they approach death. (Both he and they will enjoy great rewards as a result.) But it is the passage's images of nonsubstantiality—in the language of the sutra, three distinct images: *suimatsu* (*mizu no shibuki*, "spray"); *hō* (*awa*, "bubble"); and *en* (*hono'o*, "flickering light")—that are of greatest interest to the poem-maker. She translates *hō* and *en* into the *kago* "kagerō" and employs it (in the manner of a *makurakotoba*) as "kagerō no" with "*aru ka naki ka no yo no naka*," "this flicker-like, here-now-and-gone-in-the-next-moment world" (or "life").[88] Her

---

87. *Kokin wakashū* nos. 7 and 60 are well-known examples.

88. According to Katagiri, *kagerō* (kageroFu; earlier, *kagiroi*, i.e., kagiroFi) originally meant both a watery mist caught momentarily in light and the briefest flickering of a flame. "Will-o'-the-wisp," or *ignis fatuus*, is a rather different phenomenon, but the visual

question, "Who could have been so mistaken as to have believed (. . . *tare tanomiken*) in the notion of their own existence?" is one she asks of her readers and of herself, just as those that hear the preacher must ask it of themselves, and she knows the answer as well as they do. But when has such insight been attained? Perhaps only upon the first encounter with the quoted passage and the sutra that is its source—an encounter that changed everything that occurred thereafter, including the shape and tenor of this discourse.

"The bodhisattva" in the topic-passage of poem 43 is a being who "holds the Dharma Blossom"[89]: such a being, who accepts and preaches the *Lotus*, is so purified by it that his physical body is able to reflect everything else around him in perfect clarity. (Based on the Chinese, the last line of the quoted passage might be better translated "whatever is in the world *is visible within* his own body.") Once again, it is to the simile that the poet is drawn, but she alters its role. When the poem-speaker takes the mirror in her own hand, she is dismayed by the accuracy of the reflection she sees in it: her imperfections (whatever they may be) are perfectly revealed, and she feels ashamed (*hazukashi*). The poem itself is

---

effect is similar. The phrase "*Kagerō no aru ka naki ka no . . . yo*" recurs, for example, in *Gosen wakashū* no. 1192:

> aware to mo ushi to mo iwaji
>   kagerō no aru ka naki ka ni kenuru yo nareba
> I shall not say that it is pathetic or sad,
>   this flickering world that disappears before one can tell whether it exists
>   or not.

and no. 1265:

> yo no naka to iitsuru mono wa
>   kagerō no aru ka naki ka no hodo ni zo arikeru
> That which I have called "this world"
>   turns out to be a mere flickering that scarcely seems to exist at all.

(*SKT* 1, 59, 61; Katagiri, *Utamakura utakotoba jiten*, 102). A similar structure can be found in *Kokin wakashū* no. 731:

> kagerō no sore ka aranu ka
>   harusame no furuhi to nareba sode zo nurenuru
> Today spring rains so light that one can hardly tell that they are there are
>   falling,
>   and so my sleeves are very, very wet.

(*SKT* 1, 24.)

89. *T* 9, p. 50a; Hurvitz, *Scripture of the Lotus Blossom*, 275.

like a mirror, for its two parts, divided by the caesura after *hazukashiki*, seem to reflect one another, each with the word *kumori* ("cloud," a fuzziness or fault in the reflection) and *kagami* ("mirror"), but with a slight distortion as their syntactic relationship is rearranged. Likewise, the poem is a distorted reflection of the passage upon which it reflects. The poet's appropriation of the mirror image leads her away from the purport of its original context; the image becomes the central feature of a poem that once again reveals self-doubt and anxiety. The poem-speaker cannot fully identify with "the bodhisattva," for she does not deem herself as pure as he. Yet her utterance implies the desire for change.

> *Jōfukyō bosatsu hon* ("The Bodhisattva Never Disparaging")

> (44) ". . . for millions and millions of myriads of *kalpa*s,
>   Whose number cannot even be discussed.
>   Then at last they were enabled to hear
>   This Scripture of the Dharma Blossom."[90]

> *ika ni shite ōku no kō o tsukushiken*
> *katsu kite dani mo akanu minori o*[91]
> How did they manage to survive for so many *kalpa* without
>   it?—
> this scripture of which one cannot hear enough!

> *Nyorai jinriki hon* ("The Supernatural Powers of the Thus Come One")

> (45) "As the bright light of the sun and moon
>   Can clear away all darkness and obscurity,
>   So this man, going through the world,
>   Can extinguish the darkness of the beings."[92]

> *sayakanaru tsuki no hikari no terasazu wa*
> *kuraki michi o ya hitori yukamashi*

---

90. *T* 9, p. 52c; Hurvitz, ibid., 284.

91. The poem is reproduced here as it appears in the Matsudaira Bunko copy (Ishihara, *Hosshin wakashū no kenkyū*, 24, 54, 226). The Hashimoto edition in *SKT* has *gō*, "karma," in place of *kō*, "kalpa."

92. *T* 9, p. 52b; Hurvitz, *Scripture of the Lotus Blossom*, 290.

Were the clear light of this bright moon not shining,
    I would be all alone as I travel on this dark path.

Zokurui hon ("Entrustment")

(46) In this way, thrice stroking the bodhisattva-mahāsattvas
on the head, he said . . .[93]

itadaki o nadete oshieshi nori nareba
    kore yori kami wa aranu narikeri
This is a dharma he taught stroking the crown of their heads,
    so surely there can be no teaching that tops this!

These three topic-and-poem pairs show the poet crafting *waka* out of
passages cut very roughly from their original contexts but with an eye to
what they offer her poem-making process. Hurvitz's translation of the
couplet preceding the two that constitute the topic-text for poem 44 is,
"Age upon age they accepted and held scriptural canons like these,"
which provides a grammatical subject ("they") for what follows; in the
Chinese, the subject is explicit only in a still earlier line. The speaker of
these lines is the Buddha, telling how Sadāparibhūta (*Jōfugyō*, "Never
Disparaging")—the Buddha himself, in a former life—preached to a vast
assembly through an immeasurably long span of time, at the end of which
the assembly was finally able to hear the *Lotus* itself. The poem appears to
be a straightforward expression of awe for the singular importance of the
Lotus, emphasized by reiterating the sense that it was a very long time in
coming, and the poet seizes on the language of "time" and its measure to
formulate her poem. The imponderable *oku oku man kō*, "hundreds of
millions of *kalpa*," is translated plainly into *ōku no kō*, "many *kalpa*," with
perhaps an intentional play in the shift of initial vowel sounds from "*oku*"
to "*ōku*." *Kō o tsukusu*, "living through *kalpa*," is reminiscent of the
"Mitarashigawa tortoise" poem's first five, "*gō o tsukusu*," "living out my
karmic destiny."[94] The poem's third seven-syllable section, reproduced
here as it is by both Ishihara and Hashimoto, may mean "even when one
comes to it [the scripture, *minori*] like this," which would seem to allude to

---

93. *T* 9, p. 52c; Hurvitz, ibid., 291.

94. As noted above, Hashimoto's version, reading ". . . *gō o tsukushiken* . . ." makes the
    two poems seem even more similar. But *ōku no kō* seems the more likely form of
    adaptation and response to the topic-text's *oku oku man kō*.

some less than ideal circumstance or condition of the "hearer," but some modern printed versions read *"katsu kiku dani mo,"* which would mean "even when one hears it like this" or "when one hears just a part of it."[95] (The faultily transcribed phrase has not been worked into the translation above.) The poem-speaker seems to differentiate her experience from that of the assembly: though perhaps disadvantaged or handicapped herself (in some unspecified way), she has nonetheless learned how wonderful the teaching is, and her desire to embrace it is insatiable. The way she expresses the idea of "not having enough" or "never tiring of" the yearned-for and much-needed teaching, in *akanu*, gives the poem a strong link to the conventional topos of unquenchable yearning for the sight and sound of beloved objects, as in Narihira's *"akanaku ni madaki no tsuki no kakururu ka . . ."* (discussed above[96]) or in such earlier poems as *Man'yōshū* nos. 36–37, where Hitomaro says "though I gaze and gaze at the palace (or the river), I do not tire *(miredomo akanu)."*[97]

The passage quoted from the *gātha* that concludes the *Nyorai jinriki hon* provides for a return to the imagery of light dispersing darkness. The "man" who is said to have the capacity to shed illumination throughout the world is one who upholds and preaches the *Lotus* after the Buddha's own extinction. Here the poet's response to the simile that pairs the illumination such a man provides with that shed so widely by the sun and moon is yet another situating of the poem-speaker within a landscape where darkness has given way to light: specifically, it is the moon, pure and radiant *(sayakanaru)* in the night sky—or, more literally, "easily discerned," because its light is so strong and unobstructed—that has become the traveler's companion and now shows her the way. This poem shares its imaginary landscape—the dark path onto which the rays of moonlight fall, and a woman finding her way into the light—with Izumi Shikibu's "from darkness into darkness" poem as well as with this cycle's poems 12 and 31. But here, the scripture itself is the source of the illumination, the medium through which the benevolent Buddha sheds his light upon all beings, and the poem-speaker is relieved to find that she, too, can share it.

---

95. See Tokiwa Daijō et al., eds., *Shakkyō kaei zenshū* 1 (1936; reprinted Osaka: Tōhō Shuppan, 1978), 200; and Washio Junkei et al., eds., *Kokubun Tōhō Bukkyō sōsho* 8 (Tokyo: Tōhō Shoin, 1925), 25.

96. See part one, n. 27.

97. See Takagi Ichinosuke, Gomi Tomohide, and Ōno Susumu, eds., *NKBT* 4, 30–31.

The fragmentary prose-passage quoted as the topic of no. 46 is the introduction to a substantial discourse in which "he," the Buddha, "entrusts" the *Lotus* to "incalculable bodhisattva-mahāsattvas."[98] Yet, even in this brief fragment the poet finds what she needs for poem making: she reproduces the gesture of the stroking of the heads (*itadaki*) and then introduces another word for "head," *kami*, that allows for a rather serious play on words (the most overt such play in the cycle). The latter portion of the poem can be read "there were no other heads than these" (that is, the bodhisattva-mahāsattvas were the only ones to whom the *Lotus* could be entrusted), but, since *kami* can also mean "the top," "the ultimate," its sense as "there is nothing that is higher than this" intervenes, suggesting "there could be nothing of greater significance [than this act]" as well as "there can be nothing superior to the *Lotus*." The same passage would seem to be the topic for Kintō's poem on the "*Zokurui hon*" in his *nijūhappon no uta* of 1002 (*Kintō shū* no. 281):

> *itadaki o kaesugaesu zo kakinazuru*
> *egataki nori no ushirometasa yo*[99]
> He stroked their heads again and again:
> what grave concern he had for this rare dharma!

Both poets seem to have understood the stroking gesture as one that reflects the great importance attached to this scripture (*nori*) by the Buddha, and both rendered elements of the passage into simple declamatory verse. But Senshi's poem is perhaps the more striking because of its play on *kami*, which conveys her perception of the significance of the passage (and the gesture it describes) even as it calls attention to itself as a clever trick (as does the play on *kokoro* in poem 5).

Yakuō bosatsu hon[100] ("The Former Affairs of the Bodhisattva Medicine King")

(47) "If a woman, hearing this Chapter of the Former Affairs of the Bodhisattva Medicine King, can accept and keep it, she shall put an end to her female body, and shall never again receive one."[101]

---

98. *T* 9, p. 52c; Hurvitz, *Scripture of the Lotus Blossom*, 291.

99. *SKT* 3, 305.

100. The full title of the chapter is *Yakuō bosatsu honji hon*.

101. *T* 9, p. 54c; Hurvitz, *Scripture of the Lotus Blossom*, 300.

mareranaru nori o kikitsuru michi shi areba
    uki o kagiri to omoikeru ka na
Since there is, after all, a way for me to hear this rare dharma,
    I know that there is an end to all my sorrows.

Myōon bosatsu hon ("The Bodhisattva Fine Sound")

(48) "[Whoever is] . . . in any other troublesome place, he can rescue them all. Even in the inner quarters of a king's palace, changing into a female body, he preaches this scripture."[102]

kakubakari itou ukimi o kimi nomi zo
    nori no tame ni to narikawarikeru
Only you, Bodhisattva Fine Sound, would change into a
    despicable, sorry body like this one,
    for the dharma's sake.

The *dai* for nos. 47 and 48 reintroduce the topos of gender transformation, previously encountered most explicitly in no. 16 but related to the recurring topos of the obstacles faced by women in the path to Buddhahood. The passage, taken from the Buddha's discourse in prose in the "Medicine King" chapter, enunciates an idea of great importance to devout women: it prescribes a practical way for them to earn the same miraculous transformation achieved so magically by the Nāga girl in the "Devadatta" chapter, and the poem-speaker rejoices in her appropriation of this message. "*Nori*" here can mean this particular passage and its teaching, the chapter that contains it, and the sutra as a whole, all of which she has been able to encounter: that encounter, to which the text itself bears witness, is expressed by *kikitsuru*, (echoing the character for "hear," *mon/kik[u]*, in the quotation), which modifies *michi*, "way," suggesting "a means [of access]" or "an opportunity [for hearing]" as well as "devout practice [of which I have heard]." But, for the poem-speaker, the provision of a prescription for putting an "end to her female body" means that she, too, can expect her suffering (*uki*) to end ("*uki o kagiri to omo [u]*"). In sharp contrast to the preceding poem's treatment of its topic-text (and the poet's general tendency to treat quotations as independent texts), this poem seems to embrace the sense of the lines that follow those that are quoted. In the sutra,

---

102. *T* 9, p. 56a; Hurvitz, ibid., 308.

this passage continues with the explanation that a woman who hears the *Lotus* and "practices it as preached shall be . . . reborn on a jeweled throne among lotus blossoms, never again to be tormented by greed, never again to be tormented by anger or folly, never again to be tormented by pride, envy, or other defilements."[103] The implication is that such a woman will cease to have the putative female characteristics that mar and limit her capacities to achieve what men may achieve: in the Pure Land, these faults will be neutralized, which may mean that the woman herself will be, in a sense, neutered (a relieving prospect, rather than an abhorrent one, to this poem-speaker). These "defilements" may be among the referents of the word "*uki*," "sorrows" (or sources thereof) in the poem, and this possibility suggests an alternate reading of it that is more closely linked to the fuller context of the quoted passage: "They [i.e., women of past times who have] had an opportunity to hear this rare dharma, and so they knew (did they not?) that there was (or would be) an end to all their sorrows." But the poem-speaker certainly does not consider herself free from her afflictions as yet: the word *uki* marks her accepted view of her own condition, and the same word, transferred to the corporal body, as *ukimi*, "this sad, suffering body of mine" in response to references, in the next two topic-quotations, to the physical manifestations of bodhisattvas, continues to assert itself in the dialogue between those quotations and the poems that engage them.

In the next chapter of the *Lotus*, the Buddha praises "the Bodhisattva Fine Sound" (*Myōon bosatsu*, Gadgadasvara) for his willingness to go to extraordinary lengths to convey the teachings of the *Lotus* to those in need. In the passage quoted for no. 48, he says, this missionary's zeal even prompts him to undergo gender transformation in order to preach to women confined to private quarters within a royal palace. Such women, the passage implies, are truly in dire need of his preaching: they are just as unfortunate and disadvantaged as are beings in hell, "hungry ghosts," and dumb animals (enumerated just prior to the point where this quotation begins), if not more so. The poem concurs by referring to the female body (*nyoshin* in the sutra's prose) as "*kakubakari itou ukimi*," "a wretched and despicable body like this"—or, from the poem-speaker's point of view, "like mine." Again, "*nori*" encompasses the lesson that the bodhisattva preaches, the *Lotus* as a whole, and "the dharma," Buddhism itself, for the sake of which "Fine Sound" is willing to go to such amazing lengths. This topic-text gives the poet an opportunity to manipulate an inversion of the gender-transformation topos: a male being has made himself female in order to convey the dharma to women who might

---

103. *T* 9, p. 54c; Hurvitz, ibid., 300.

otherwise have no access to it—women who may have been thought to share in some sense the relative and/or symbolic isolation of the Kamo inmates.

Kanzeon bosatsu hon[104] ("The Gateway of the Bodhisattva Sound-Observer")

(49) "He is fully endowed with the power of supernatural penetration
And broadly cultivates wisdom and expedient devices;
In the lands of all ten quarters
There is no kṣetra where he does not display his body.
The various evil destinies,
Those of hell, ghosts, and beasts,
As well as the pains of birth, old age, sickness, and death,
All little by little are extinguished . . ."[105]

au koto o izuku nite to ka chigirubeki
ukimi no yukan kata o shiraneba
Where, I wonder, can he promise to meet me?
I do not know what lies ahead for this sorry self of mine.

The poet responds to these lines from the Buddha's gātha in praise of Avalokiteśvara (Kanzeon bosatsu) with a reversion to self-doubt. Although the bodhisattva is said to appear everywhere to alleviate the sufferings of all creatures, the poem-speaker wonders whether he can do so for her. Where can they have their promised encounter if the conditions of her life generate a sense of distance from, rather than proximity to, the sphere in which he functions? Somewhere (izuku nite to ka), perhaps in some "country" (setsu, from the Sanskrit kṣetra) other than this one, but who knows where that is, or what destiny will decree for the remainder of this poem-speaker's "sorry existence" (ukimi) here or in lives to come? She literally says, "Since I do not know where this ukimi is going . . ." ([ukimi no yukan kata o shiraneba], and here ukimi is the corporal body that experiences the mortal "pains" listed in the quoted passage, i.e., the present physical self), "so where can he promise to meet me?" The linking of "meet" (au) and

---

104. The full title of the chapter is Kanzeon bosatsu fumon bon.

105. T 9, p. 58a; Hurvitz, Scripture of the Lotus Blossom, 318. The following line, in Hurvitz's translation, is "By the Sound-Observer," i.e., "by Kanzeon bosatsu."

"promise" (*chigiru*) in other *waka* contexts would of course suggest romantic assignation,[106] but here they are deployed in an anxious query about a
"promised meeting" for which the poem-speaker yearns with a very special passion.

> *Darani hon* ("Dhāraṇī")

> (50) "[Be the attacker] . . . anyone in the form of . . . a boy,
> or of a girl, even in a dream: let none of these harm [these
> teachers of Dharma]!"[107]

nani to iedo yume no naka ni mo ayamataji
  nori o tamoteru hito to narinaba
No matter what I do or say, even in my dreams I shall do no
harm
    if I have become one of those who uphold this scripture.

In the *Darani* chapter, the speakers of the quoted passage are "ten
daughters of *rākṣasa*" (*rasetsunyo*—that is, daughters of demons) who
promise the Buddha to protect his *Lotus* scripture and, particularly, those
who preach it (*hōshi* or *hosshi*, "teachers of dharma") from all manner of
attack from many sorts of vicious creatures, fevers that last for various
periods, or beings who may temporarily take on mortal form as adult
males or females or as children (perhaps as a disguise). In the poem the
phrase "in dream" is translated literally (*muchū* becomes *yume no naka ni*),
but the full range of forms of possible attackers—a considerably broader
range in the sutra, narrowed in the quotation to "those who have the form
of a boy or of a girl"—is subsumed in *nani to iedomo*, "whatever it may be,"
which may also mean "whatever one says"—suggesting perhaps the desire to protect the dharma, and its protectors, from slander. *Nori o tamoteru
hito*, "a person who upholds the dharma," can be either the preachers

---

106. An early example of the association of *au* and *chigiru* in a poem that evokes the context
of "romantic encounter" can be seen in a Tanabata poem, *Kokin wakashū* no. 178
(Fujiwara Okikaze):

> *Chigirikemu kokoro zo tsuraki*
>   *tanabata no toshi ni hitotabi au wa au ka wa*
> How cruel to have pledged to meet this way,
>   like the Tanabata stars: can we call meeting only once each year "meeting"?

(*SKT* 1, 14.)

107. *T* 9, p. 59b; Hurvitz, *Scripture of the Lotus Blossom*, 323. The preceding lines, in Hurvitz's translation, are "Let anyone rather climb upon our heads than hurt these teachers of Dharma, be the attacker [any of a variety of ghastly creatures and demons]."

whom the demon-daughters swear to protect or the poem-speaker, positing herself as another female protector (as in the translation above). Likewise, *ayamataji* can be an admonitory charge to a third person—"Do ye no harm!"—or the poem-speaker's own vow, "I shall do no harm." But *ayamats[u]* is not a particularly literal interpretation of *nō/nayamasu*, the character that means "cause pain to" in the quotation: perhaps the poet read this word as an intransitive *nayamu*, "have pain/trouble" and then interpolated *ayamats[u]* in its intransitive sense, "be in error" or "be lost," yielding a poem that means something more like "no matter what happens, even in my dreams I shall not [or let me not] go astray." These ambiguities may be intentional, designed to force the reader to ponder the poem's possible range of modes of response to the quotation. What seems most clear is that the poet wishes both to reiterate the demon-daughter's sentiment and to express one on the poem-speaker's part: even in the most adverse of circumstances she will not "harm" the dharma or depart from her devotion to it. At least, she hopes, this will be so in the realm of dream, if not in reality.

> *Myōshōgon bon*[108] ("The Former Affairs of the King Fine Adornment")

> (51) "A Buddha is as hard to encounter . . . as it would be for a one-eyed tortoise to encounter a hole in a floating piece of wood. Yet, our former merits having been profound and of great proportions, we have been born into the Buddha-dharma."[109]

hitome nite tanomi kaketsuru ukigi ni wa
  norihatsurubeki kokochi ya wa suru
Do you think that in the end you will ride on it
    if you have looked in trust at that floating piece of wood
    with but one eye?

The metaphor of the one-eyed tortoise and the floating piece of wood originates in a story about two brothers, men of extraordinary insight and piety, who plead with their parents—a heretic king and his queen—for permission to become disciples of the Buddha of their time, and to be able to take vows and leave home (*shukke*) immediately, for, as they explain, it is a rare thing indeed to be born into the same age as a Buddha who

---

108. The full title of the chapter is *Myōshōgon'ō honji hon.*

109. *T* 9, p. 60a-b; Hurvitz, *Scripture of the Lotus Blossom*, 327–28.

preaches the *Lotus*—as rare as the flowering of the *uḍumbara* once every three thousand years, as unlikely as it is for a half-blind tortoise to find and mount a bit of flotsam floating in a vast sea. For the poet, who, as we know, had had occasion to compose a poem alluding to this passage at least once before, this quotation provides yet another variation on the "encounter" theme. In the "Mitarashigawa tortoise" poem, the "floating piece of wood" was made an explicit symbol of Buddhism itself—*nori no ukigi*—the sought-for object so hard for the poet to meet (*au*) face to face. Here this language is given a further twist: the verb *au*, explicit in the quotation itself, is transposed into the "*nori-*" of "*norihatsuru . . .*," "climb upon, at last"—a "*nori*" that has lost its meaning as "dharma" but reproduces the same sounds. "*Hitome*" is literally "with one eye," and if the poet compared that handicap with her own disadvantages, she may have meant her poem to be an exhortation, to others as well as to herself, to believe that, whatever difficulties may intervene, the sought-for "encounter" will inevitably occur. But "*hitome*" can also mean "the whole eye," and if this inverted meaning comes into play the poem may read, "Don't you believe that you will ride on it if you have trusted wholeheartedly in that floating piece of wood?" Even if this reading eliminates the meaning of the tortoise's "half-blindness" as intended in the brothers' plea, the poem still overlaps with the intent of the original passage, for it is still an endorsement of the notion that one must see one's opportunities and take them, or remain blind and adrift in troubled waters.

> *Fugen bosatsu bon*[110] ("The Encouragements of the Bodhisattva Universally Worthy")

> (52) "In the realm of the Buddha King Surpassing the Awe-Inspiring Excellence of Gems, I heard from afar that in this *Sahā* world-sphere the Scripture of the Dharma Blossom is preached, and with a multitude of incalculable, limitless hundreds of thousands of myriads of millions of bodhisattvas I have come to listen receptively."[111]

tazunekite nori o kikiken sono toki ni
    awade itsushika arishi wagami zo
I was not there when he came searching and then heard
    the scripture . . .

---

110. The full title of the chapter is *Fugen bosatsu kanbotsu hon*.

111. *T* 9, p. 61a; Hurvitz, *Scripture of the Lotus Blossom*, 332. "*Sahā* world sphere" refers to the mundane world, where the Buddha Śākyamuni is preaching, to which the speaker, Samantabhadra, has journeyed from the world of another Buddha.

The passage quoted from the last chapter of the *Lotus Sutra* is Saman-tabhadra's account of how he has come to yet another great "meeting" with the rare opportunity to hear the *Lotus,* and in response the poet returns to the language of "seeking out" (*tazunekite*) an encounter with the dharma (*nori*) and hearing it (*kik[u]*). The poem-speaker, however, laments that she missed that opportunity (*sono toki ni awade*). *Itsushika arishi wagami zo,* the conclusion of the poem as reproduced in Shoryōbu A, would seem to mean "when was I there?" or "when did I have that experience?": Shoryōbu B and the Matsudaira Bunko copy read あはていてありし我身そ (*awade iteru* [or *ideru*] *arishi wagami zo*), which is virtually indecipherable, for which reason the translation above has been left incomplete. But the poem is apparently another of the poet's efforts to express a difference between her own experience and the ideal experience, in this case ex-emplified by Samantabhadra's. Though she has encountered the dharma and its scriptures, and has given evidence here of that encounter, there is still another, ultimate meeting that she has yet to experience—and she wonders if she ever will.

Fugengyō: The Samantabhadra Meditation Sutra[112]

(53) All your sins can disappear, as do frost and dew
When they are touched by the warmth of sunlight;
Therefore, you should concentrate with your whole
heart
To repent the sins of the Six Senses. [113]

tsukuri okeru tsumi o ba ikade tsuyu shimo no
asahi ni ataru gotoku keshiten[114]
Is it possible that all the sins I have committed can disappear
as do dew and frost in the warmth of the morning sun?

The quotation from the "closing sutra" of the *Lotus* triad reproduces the final couplets of a *gātha* in which the Buddha recommends reading or chanting the Mahāyāna sutras as a means of purifying each of the "Six Senses" (or "Six Roots," *rokkon*[115]). The transposition of imagistic elements (as well as the verb *kes[u]*) is literal, and the poet even translates *nyo* (the

---

112. The full title of the sutra is *Kanfugen bosatsu gyōbōgyō.*

113. *T* 9, no. 227, p. 393b.

114. Shoryōbu B and the Matsudaira Bunko copy read "*asahi ni ateru gotoku keshiten* 朝日 にあてるごとくけしてん," which Ishihara prefers for its implication that the light is "actively" sought (Ishihara, *Hosshin wakashū no kenkyū,* 253–54).

115. See n. 82 (to HSWKS no. 39) on *rokkon* and *rokujin.*

third character of the first line) as *gotoku*, spelling out the explicit simile. This process is facilitated by the fact that *tsuyu*, *shimo*, and various words for the processes of vaporizing (forms of *kes[u]*) are closely linked in the *waka* lexicon, where it is also invariably the sun's light that causes the dew to evaporate or the frost to melt. The term *e'nichi*, "benevolent light" (in the second phrase of the quotation), can serve as a metaphor for "the Buddha's benevolent wisdom" (*jñāna-divākara*[116]), and the poet's translation, "the morning sun" (*asahi*), may carry that nuance. But, as elsewhere, the poet reframes the message—another exhortation to follow a particular practice and to expect specific results— as a doubting question (*ikade . . . keshiten*): "Can I realize the promised effects, too? When the 'benevolent light' that shines out of these scriptures (that I have read and written about herein) falls on me," she asks, "will the sins I have committed [*tsukuri okeru tsumi*—perhaps "sins that I am forced to commit inadvertently, by my special condition"] evaporate as quickly as do the dew and frost?" The verb *ok[u]* in *tsukuriokeru tsumi*, "crimes committed and 'inscribed' in one's life-record," is a kind of pun, since it is also used in *waka* to describe the falling or alighting of dew (*oku tsuyu*) or frost (*oku shimo*). It also prepares the way for the explicit autumnal references of the next and penultimate topic-text and poem pair. It must have been easy for Senshi to devise a poem out of such familiar autumn *waka* elements, and even the pun seems inevitable. But there is another face to this adroit manipulation, for the poem-speaker's rhetoric reveals that she is still uncertain about the validity of this particular scriptural message in her own case.

Nehan[gyō]: The Nirvana Sutra

(54) For example, as, in the tilling of fields,
　　　The tilling in autumn produces the richest yield,
　　　This scripture, in the same way,
　　　Is the richest among all scriptures.[117]

aki no ta no kaesugaesu mo kanashiki wa
　　kagiri no tabi no minori narikeri[118]
So very sad indeed, as are the barren autumn fields, turned
　　and turned again,
　　is this last-given dharma, these final fruits.

---

116. Mochizuki, *Bukkyō daijiten* 1, 285c.

117. *T* 12, no. 374, p. 385a.

118. Reproduced here as in Shoryōbu A. Shoryōbu B reads ". . . *kanashi* □ *wa* . . . かなし は "; the Shimbara copy reads ". . . *kanashisa wa* . . . . かなしさは ."

As the *Nirvana Sutra* follows the *Lotus* in Tendai and other chronologies, as an essential afterthought, culminating and concluding the Buddha's life and career, so does the quotation from it here follow after the completion of the *Lotus* quotation-and-poem sequence. The autumnal imagery of this self-descriptive passage (the Buddha's own characterization of his final discourse) falls into the same seasonal context as that of the "dew and frost" of the preceding pair, creating a graceful link between the two pairs and also allowing the poet to invoke the context and association of autumn and harvest, the closing of the agricultural cycle, as she approaches the close of the cycle of poems. Cued by the simple but rich simile in the quotation, the poet elaborates its image into a complex structure. Once again, the key word around which the poem's double contexts revolve is *minori* (i.e., *minōri*), "the holy dharma," but also suggestive, in this context, of "ripened grain," "the fruits of the field" (also *minōri*). These autumn fields (*aki no ta*) have been "turned" (*kaesu*) yet again, after the harvest of the grain, and their furrows lie fallow. (*Kaesu* is the poet's transposition of the verb "to cultivate," "till with a spade," *kō/tagayas[u]*.) This barren scene is sad to look upon—as is the scene of the Buddha's demise, so elaborately described in the sutra—but its description serves as a preface (*jo*) to the word *kaesugaesu*, an intensifying modifier for *kanashi*, "terribly, terribly sad." What is truly sad, the poem-speaker thus declares, is this "last harvesting of the ripened grain" (*kagiri no tabi no minori*), that is, this last occasion on which the Buddha's wisdom is imparted to those whose spiritual nourishment depends on him. The poet's conversion of the imagery of the fields from richness to barrenness embodies her role in the discourse between scripture and *waka*: appropriating the imagery she encounters, she responds, perhaps characteristically, not by reproducing its sense of final fulfillment but by invoking a scene and mood of desolation. The result is perhaps more easily recognizable as an autumnal poem than a less gloomy poem might be, and it marks an intentional reversion to the cycle's recurring pessimistic strain.

> (55) "We beg to take this merit
> And spread it universally to all,
> And with the living beings
> All together achieving the Buddha Path."[119]

> *ikani shite shiru mo shiranu mo yo no hito o*
> *hachisu no ue no tomo to nashiten*

---

119. *T* 9, p. 42c; Hurvitz, *Scripture of the Lotus Blossom*, 143.

How can I cause everyone, the knowing and the unknowing
   alike,
   to be companions, all together, upon the lotus?

The source of the final topic-quotation is not cited as it is in every other
pair, which suggests that this pair is to be read not only as a discourse
between this particular passage and this poem, but also as a summary
epilogue for the cycle in its entirety—or, perhaps, as something like a
hanka, the reiterative coda (in *tanka* form) that follows many of the longer
poems (*chōka*) in the *Man'yōshū.* The source, in fact, is the "*Kejōyu hon*" of
the *Lotus Sutra,* the chapter that provided the topic-quotation for poem 31:
here, the topic-text is the last two couplets of a *gātha* said to have been
sung by millions of "Brahma god kings" (*Bonten'ō*) after reverencing the
Buddha of their time and presenting him with many fabulous offerings,
including celestial flowers piled as high as Mount Sumeru itself.[120] The
kings pray for the transfer of their rewards (*kudoku*) for these gestures to
all other beings, to enable one and all to attain Buddhahood (. . . *jōbutsu-
dō*). The poet appropriates this prayer (*negawaku wa* . . .) to declaim the
same intent as does the "prayer" (*negawaku wa* . . .) at the end of the
preface to the cycle. Her goal, she says here, is (as in the preface) to share
the benefits of her meritorious deeds with others, whether they "know all
that there is to know" or are, like herself, still in the process of learning—
but how is this to be done? All of the copies of the cycle present this
inquiry in alternate forms: the version reproduced above is that of the
main text of both Shoryōbu A and B and of the Matsudaira Bunko copy,
but all three also have a parallel line (inserted just to the right and slightly
above the corresponding section, and in a slightly smaller hand, in the
Matsudaira Bunko copy, and just to the left in the Shoryōbu copies):

hotoke no michi ni sasoiireten
How can I cause everyone . . . to follow my lead into the
   Buddha's Path?

This ending is obviously a much closer rendition of the language of the
quotation, while the other ending may represent the author's attempt to
recast the original passage while retaining its essential intent and repeat-
ing the same valedictory that closes the "Four Vast Vows," the "Ten Great
Vows," and the preface, which also emulates them. And while either
ending provides the cycle with a kind of closure in the return to this

---

120. Ibid.

formal valedictory gesture, it is perhaps significant that the poem, constituted either way, is still a question, a gesture that leaves the cyclical discourse (conducted in almost exactly the same language in previous poems, especially nos. 3 and 13) open to further development. The poet ends her cycle not with a closing, affirming -*keri* or a full-stop -*ka na*, but with a querying, open-ended -*mu* (written -*n*). The query, of course, has an obvious answer: this cycle of poems on passages from the scripture, reflecting and recasting those passages as new *waka* utterances, is the embodiment and realization of the prayer, the vehicle whereby the poet has attempted to convey her readers toward the goal they all share. It is this very text—itself a meshing of many texts—that will show them all the way out of their darkness toward the Pure Land's brilliant light. Yet, in her final utterance, the poem-speaker does not declare this outright: rather, she asks herself, and her reader, if it is indeed so. For the present, she cannot know whether the writing and reading of this text will indeed have its sought-for effect in her own destiny or in the destined futures of those with whom she wishes to share it: she can only continue to pray that it will.

EPILOGUE

In the reading of *Hosshin wakashū* carried out here I have gone to some length to emphasize its cyclical character, to show what effects are achieved by the poet and impressed upon the reader as the cycle turns from topic-text to topic-text, as its composer moves among a set of recurring attitudes and reverts to recurring diction, to underlying themes and motifs that are brought to the surface as those texts and the responses they prompt may dictate. We must recognize, however, that the ways these poems are most likely to have been read in the past would not have called as much attention to such characteristics as they have been given here. Medieval readers, whose reading was invariably shaped by the *chokusenshū* editors, were much more likely to encounter but one or two of the poems at a time, most often classed with others like them as responses to scriptural topic-texts (in some cases, the same or related texts), and therefore read them as examples of a genre, "*Shakkyōka*"—as representatives of one poet's exercise in that genre to be compared and associated with others apparently like it. Removed from its cyclical context and placed in a generic one, a single poem from *Hosshin wakashū*, or two or three, juxtaposed with other "Buddhist poems," inevitably would produce a very different set of impressions: each poem would become a free-standing record (among similar records) of its particular author's singular encounter with an isolated scriptural text, and any gesture to other poems that the single poem might appear to make would have to be seen as a gesture to other poems in the whole *waka* corpus, or in the *Shakkyōka* genre, rather than to other poems within the organic entity in which it was originally conceived. A reading of *Hosshin wakashū* as a cycle, however, suggests that its poems make both kinds of gestures, as well as gestures to the poems within that cycle itself.

As reading contexts were shifted and rearranged through time, the potential range of ways of reading poems like those in *Hosshin wakashū* multiplied, but the range of readings likely to be practiced was diminished. To be sure, the reading of such poems in their anthologized contexts may have been largely responsible for preserving knowledge of the texts that originally incorporated them, and perhaps insured the preservation of those texts themselves, in later copies. But it also meant that encounters with those poems in their whole original frames would be greatly outnumbered by encounters in the new frames that the anthologies gave them. The rare reader who made his or her way through the entire cycle would thereby reenact the whole series of encounters between scriptural texts and *waka* texts recorded there, but the reader who was presented with just one of those encounters would know it perhaps only as a representative selection of that larger and more complex series of encounters, or simply as an isolated encounter associable with the similar encounters of other earlier and later poets, enacted intermittently through time. In this way, anthologized reading replaced one sense of the poem's possible or imaginable relationship to the poet's consciousness and experience with another, perhaps equally as valid or invalid, but certainly different.

Of course, Senshi herself was a reader of *chokusenshū* and other collections, and she was probably sensitive to the different effects of the reading practices of her own time. Perhaps she even anticipated that some of her *Hosshin wakashū* poems might be taken out of their original frame and worked into anthologies, and then be read in the new contexts decreed there. Before that, however, there must have been some among those denizens of the Saiin, the probable first readers of *Hosshin wakashū*, who read it in its entirety and, in their own way, charted its cyclical paths. But there must also have been occasions when they focused on just one or just a few of the poems, voicing the sounds, examining the shapes, and considering the poem or poems as models for their own creative efforts in a similar vein. In such readings, intense scrutiny must have fallen on each poem's formal aspects, the discrete elements of its diction, and the precise character of its links to its topic-text—and, perhaps, to its significance as defined by the context of the scriptural text and its own inherent significances. And one additional factor must have done much to shape the context of those early readings: whether a woman in service in the Saiin read the work in its entirety or only a segment or segments of it, she would certainly have read it as the creation of a real person whom she personally knew, with whom she shared the routines of daily life, a person whose poetic sensibilities and skills she admired and emulated, and a person she regarded as mentor in the ways of poetry, in the ways of religion, and in such intersections of those "ways" as *Hosshin wakashū* itself marks. Such a reader could readily feel the impact of reenacting her mistress's own intense encounters with scripture, would readily identify with her responses, and would appropriate her mistress's sentiments as her own. She might feel a new awe for her mistress's accomplishments and gain a new awareness of the dimensions of her faith, and be inspired to strive still harder to emulate her. The cycle would thus realize its professed purpose.

Before long, however, the immediacy and intimacy of such reading would be irretrievable. When they could, the latter-day *chokusenshū* editors would always try to recapture something of that intimate way of reading, by giving their readers, in *kotobagaki*, whatever "information" they had about the poems they were about to read and about how the poet wrote them, so as to make readings that involve or are dependent upon a consciousness of the poet's persona possible, or inevitable. They thus replaced the intensity of reading experiences that once occurred within intimate social contexts with an intense nostalgia for those contexts as they reimagined them. Historical or pseudo-historical personality, thus enshrined, remains deeply embedded in the *waka* reading tradition, for better or for worse, occasionally transcending or displacing the very poems its evocation is intended to illuminate. We have seen how *setsuwa* and *rekishi-monogatari* narratives shaped a persona for the poet Senshi and influenced some readings of her works, and we have at times allowed that tradition to shape our own reading of *Hosshin wakashū*. Still, let it be remembered that *Hosshin wakashū*, as originally conceived and originally encountered by its readers, was read, in whole or in part, in the context of fully shared experience and understanding, and that the cycle itself was created as something new to be shared, both as an exemplary exercise of the art of *waka* and as a devotional vehicle through which its writer and readers could be borne beyond the limiting conditions of their lives toward a spiritual ideal that beckoned from afar. The medium was of two distinct languages, and the text formed by their interaction was one that constantly, through its form and content, announced itself to be both literary and pietistic and implied that no distinction need be drawn between the two. As the two languages met in a display of their differences as well as their points of contact, so did the secular world of *waka* and the idealized sphere of Buddhism converge. Though absorbed with and fully demonstrative of difference, then, these "Buddhist poems" also showed collectively that the exploration of difference might also be a means toward its diminution and its replacement by a merging of the differentiated: Chinese text met Japanese text, the way of *waka* became the way of the Buddha, and writer and readers, though perhaps still formally constrained, joined with the rest of society in enactment of their Buddhist faith.

APPENDIX
THE TEXT OF
HOSSHIN WAKASHŪ

発心和歌集

妾久係念於仏陀常寄情法宝為菩提也、釈尊説法華一乗歌詠諸如来

之善、爰知歌詠之功高為仏事焉、猶梵語者天竺之詞流沙逥隔、漢

字者震旦之跡風俗各殊、弟子誕生皇朝受身婦女、不兼邯鄲之歩偏

染桑梓之情、是故素菱之新詠卅一字歌学而述其義、飢人之始献卅

一字様習而以其詞、始四弘願海乎十大願、惣五十五首勒為一巻、

名曰発心和歌集、是則所以十方浄土之際、遍発往生之心九品蓮台

之上、終殖化生之縁也、何必傾力営堂塔教主懇誓願之誠、何必剃

髪入山林経生新讃歎之徳耶、不知出此和歌之道入彼阿字之門矣、

唯願若有見聞者生生世世与妾値遇多宝如来之願、定有誹謗者在在

所所与妾結縁同不軽菩薩之行、一心至実三宝捨諸、嗟乎秋風吹之

声是告老、晩日衝山之景非偸命哉、泣思照鑑乎執此時、于時寛弘

九載南呂也

衆生無辺誓願度

一 たれとなくひとつにのりのいかだにてかなたの岸に着くよしもがな

煩悩無辺誓願断

二 かぞふべき方もなけれど身に近きまづはいつつのさはりなりける

法門無尽誓願知

三 いかにしてつくしてしらんさとること入ること難き門ときけども

無上菩提誓願証

四 このしな咲きひらくなる蓮葉のうへの上なる身ともならばや

Hosshin wakashū preface, 1–4

般若心経
色即是空、空即是色、受想行識、亦復如是

五　世世をへてときくる法はおほかれど是ぞまことの心なりける
普賢十願
礼敬諸仏
普賢行願威神力、普現一切如来前、一身復現刹塵身、一一遍礼刹
塵仏

六　きみだにもちりのなかにも顕ればたつとゐるとぞゐやまはるべき
称讃如来
各以一切音声海、普於無量妙言詞、尽於未来一切劫、讃仏深心功
徳海

七　おもふにもいふにもあまるふかさにてことも心も及ばれぬかな
広修供養
我以広大勝解心、深信一切三世仏、悉以普賢行願力、普通供養諸
如来

八　さしながら三世のほとけに奉る春咲く花も秋のもみぢも
懺悔業障
我昔所造諸悪業、皆由無始貪瞋痴、従身語意之所生、一切我今皆
懺悔

九　年ごろぞつきせざりける我が身より人のためまでなげきつづくる
随喜功徳
十方一切諸如来、二乗有学及無学、一切如来与菩薩、所有功徳皆
随喜

一〇　ちかくてもとほくききてもこのかたはなごりなくこそあらはれにけれ

Hosshin wakashū 5–10

請転法輪

十方所有世間灯、最初成就菩提者、我今一切皆勧請、転於無上妙
法輪

一一　のちまでもひろめてしかなかへるとて法の契をむすびおきする

諸仏住世

諸仏若欲示涅槃、我志至誠而勧請、唯願久住刹塵劫、利益一切諸
衆生

一二　みな人のひかりをあふぐ空の月のどかに照せ雲がくれせで

常随仏学

我随一切如来覚、修習普賢円満行、供養過去諸如来、及与現在十
方仏

一三　いかにしてのりをたもたむよにふれば眠もさめぬ夢の悲しさ

恒順衆生

我常随順諸衆生、尽於未来一切劫、恒修普賢広大門、円満無上大
菩提

一四　うれしきもつらきもことに別れぬは人にしたがふこころなりけり

普皆廻向

我此普賢殊勝行、無辺勝福皆廻向、普願沈溺諸衆生、即往無量光
仏刹

一五　かくばかりそこひもしらぬわがやみにしづまん人をうかべてしかな

転女成仏経

消滅先罪業、当得大菩薩、果転女身、成無上道

一六　とりわきてとかれし法にあひぬれば身もかへつべく聞くぞ嬉しき

Hosshin wakashū 11–16

如意輪経
阿弥陀仏、自現其身、見極楽界、種種荘厳

一七 ここながらかしこのかざり顕はるるときぞ心のごとくなりける

阿弥陀経
池中蓮華大如車輪、青色青光、黄色黄光、赤色赤光、白色白光、
微妙香潔

一八 いろいろのはちすかかやく池水にかなふこころやすみて見ゆらん

於諸仏土随願往生、乃至菩提不堕悪趣
理趣分

一九 いづる日のあした毎には人しれずにしにこころは入るとならなん

仁王経上巻
世諦幻化起、譬如虚空花

二〇 おほ空に咲きたるはなの吹くかぜに散るを我が身によそへてぞみる

同経下巻
有本自無、因縁成諸、盛者必衰、実者必虚

二一 はかなくもたのみけるかなはじめより有るにもあらぬ世にこそ有りけれ

本願薬師経
一聞我名、悪病除愈、乃至速証、無上菩提

二二 ひとたびも聞くには御名ぞたもたるる思ひわづらふ我が名なれども

寿命経
若人毎日為一切衆生転読此経、終无天死短命之怖

二三 よそ人のためにたもてる法故に数ならぬ身に程はへぬらん

Hosshin wakashū 17–23

無量義経
戒定恵解知見生、三昧六通道品発、慈悲十力無畏起、衆生善業因
縁出

二四 かくばかり人の心にまかせけるほとけのたねをもとめけるかな
法華経
序品

二五 ぬる夜なくのりを求めし人も有るを夢の中にて過す身ぞうき
方便品
又見仏子、未嘗睡眠、経行林中、勤求仏道

二六 ひとたびの花のかをりをしるべにてむすの仏にあひみざらめや
若人散乱心、乃至以一花、供養於画像、漸見無数仏

二七 あまたありと門をば聞きて出でしかどひとつの法のくるまなりけり
譬喩品
羊車鹿車、大牛之車、今在門外、汝等出来

二八 草の庵にとしへし程の心には露かからんとおもひかけきや
信解品
示其金銀、真珠頗梨、諸物出入、皆使令知、猶処門外、止宿草菴

二九 ひとつ色に我が身うつれど花の色もにしにさすえや匂ひますらん
薬草喩品
譬如大雲、以一味雨、潤於人花、各得成実

三〇 のりおもふ心しふかく成りぬれば露の空にもすずしかりけり
授記品
若知我深心、見為授記者、如以甘露灑、除熱得清涼

Hosshin wakashū 24–30

化城喩品
長夜増悪趣、減損諸天衆、従冥入於冥、永不聞仏名

三一　くらきより暗きにながく入りぬとも尋ねて誰にとはんとすらん

五百弟子授記品
以無価宝殊、繋着内衣裏、嘿与而捨去、時臥不覚知

三二　ゐひのうちにかけし衣のたまたまもむかしの友にあひてこそしれ

授学無学人記品
世尊慧灯明、我聞授記音、心歓喜充満、如甘露見灌

三三　あきらけきのりの灯なかりせばこころのやみのいかではれまし

法師品
寂寞無人声、読誦此経典、我爾時為現、清浄光明身

三四　空すみて心のどけきさ夜なかに有明の月のひかりをぞます

見宝塔品
釈迦牟尼仏、以右指開、七宝塔戸、出大音声

三五　玉の戸をひらきし時にあはずして明けぬよにしもまどふべしやは

提婆達多品
皆遥見彼、竜女成仏、普為時会、人天説法、心大歓喜

三六　さはりにもさはらぬためし有りければ隔つる雲もあらじとぞ思ふ

勧持品
為説是経故、忍此諸難事、我不愛身命、但惜無上道

三七　うきことのしのび難きをしのびてもなほこの道ををしみとどめん

安楽行品
在於閑処、修摂其心、安住不動、如須弥山

三八　さだめなきよも何ならず法を思ふこころのうちしうごきなければ

Hosshin wakashū 31–38

従地湧出品
善学菩薩道、不染世間法、如蓮華在水、従地而湧出

三九　いさぎよき人の道にも入りぬればむつの塵にもけがれざりけり
如来寿量品
為度衆生故、方便現涅槃、而実不滅度、常住此説法、我常住於
此、以諸神通力、令顚倒衆生、雖近而不見

四〇　そのかみの心まどひの名残にてちかきを見ぬぞわびしかりける
分別功徳品
雨天曼陀羅、摩訶曼陀羅、釈梵如恒沙、無数仏土来、雨栴檀沈
水、繽紛而乱墜、如鳥飛空下、供散於諸仏

四一　いろいろの花ちりくれば雲井より飛びかふ鳥と見えまがひけん
随喜功徳品
世皆不牢固、如水沫泡焔、汝等咸応当、疾生厭離心

四二　かげろふの有るかなきかの世の中にわれあるものとたれ頼みけん
法師功徳品
又如浄明鏡、悉見諸色像、菩薩於浄身、皆見世所有

四三　くもりなきかがみのうちぞはづかしきかがみのかげのくもりなければ
常不軽菩薩品
億億万劫、至不可議、時乃得聞、是法花経

四四　いかにしておほくのごふを尽しけむかつきてだにもあかぬみのりを
如来神力品
如日月光明、能除諸幽冥、斯人行世間、能滅衆生闇

四五　さやかなる月のひかりのてらさずはくらき道をや独ゆかまし

Hosshin wakashū 39–45

嘱累品
如是三摩諸菩薩、頂而作是言

四六 いただきをなでてをしへし法なれば是よりかみはあらぬなりけり

薬王菩薩品
若有女人、聞是薬王菩薩本事品、能受持者、尽是女身、後不復受

四七 まれらなるのりを聞きつる道しあればうきをかぎりと思ひけるかな

妙音菩薩品
及衆難処、皆能救済、乃於王後宮、変為女身、而説是経

観世音菩薩品
具足神通力、広修知方便、十方諸国土、無刹不現身、種種諸悪
趣、地獄鬼畜生、生老病死苦、以漸悉令滅

四八 かくばかりいとふうき身を君のみぞのりの為にと成りかはりける

四九 あふことをいづくにてとか契るべきうき身のゆかん方をしらねば

陀羅尼品
若童男形、若童女形、乃至夢中、亦復莫悩

五〇 なにといへど夢のなかにもあやまたじ法をたもてる人と成りなば

妙荘厳王品
又如一眼之亀、値浮木孔、而我等宿福深厚、生値仏法

五一 ひとめにてたのみかけつる浮木には乗りはつるべき心地やはする

普賢菩薩品
宝威徳上王仏国、遥聞此娑婆世界、説法華経与無量无辺、百千万
億菩薩衆、共来聴受

五三 たづねてのりを聞きけんその時にあはでいつしかありし我が身そ

Hosshin wakashū 46–52

普賢経
衆罪如霜露、慧日能消除、是故応至心、懺悔六情恨

五三　つくりおける罪をばいかで露霜の朝日にあたるごとくけしてん

涅槃経
譬如耕田秋暇為勝、此経如是諸経中勝

五四　秋の田のかへすがへすもかなしきはかぎりのたびの御法なりける

願以此功徳、普及於一切、我等与衆生、皆共成仏道

五五　いかにしてしるもしらぬもよの人を蓮のうへのともとなしてん

Hosshin wakashū 53–55

List of Characters for Japanese and Chinese Names and Terms

Items are listed in alphabetical order. Names of persons and places, titles of texts, and specialized or technical terms are included. Most items normally written in kana (eg., *aware*) are not included in the list. Titles of texts are in italics. For titles, terms, and other elements of the text of *Hosshin wakashū* itself, see the reproduction of the printed text in the appendix.

aishō　哀傷

aji [no mon]　阿字［之門］

Akazome Emon　赤染衛門

ama　あま, 尼

Amida　阿弥陀

Amida hijiri　阿弥陀聖

Amidakyō　阿弥陀経

anokutara sanmyaku
　sanbodaishin
　阿耨多羅三藐三菩提心

Ariwara Narihira　在原業平

Asagao　朝顔

asedono　汗殿

Bai Juyi　白居易

betsu imikotoba　別忌詞

Biwa (lake)　琵琶

Bodaikō　菩提講

Bodaishin o hossu　菩提心を発す

bonnō　煩悩

Bonnō　梵王

Bonten'ō　梵天王

Bosatsu　菩薩

Buppōsō　仏法僧

Butsu　仏

Chōgen [era]　長元

151

chokusenshū　勅撰集

dai　題

daiei　題詠

Daigo　醍醐

Daihannyaharamittakyō
大般若波羅蜜多経

Daisaiin　大斎院

Daisaiin gyoshū　大斎院御集

Daisaiin saki no gyoshū
大斎院前の御集

daiseshu　大施主

Dajōdaijin　太政大臣

dō　堂

Eiga monogatari　榮花物語

Engi shiki　延喜式

Enpō [era]　延宝

Enryakuji　延暦寺

En'yū　円融

fudan nenbutsu　不断念仏

Fūga wakashū　風雅和歌集

Fugen bosatsu　普賢菩薩

Fugen bosatsu gyōgansan
普賢菩薩行願讚

Fugen bosatsu kanbotsu hon
普賢菩薩勘発品

Fugen jūgan　普賢十願

Fujiwara Akisuke　藤原顕輔

Fujiwara Anshi　藤原安子

Fujiwara Arikuni　藤原有国

Fujiwara Kanemichi　藤原兼道

Fujiwara Kanesuke　藤原兼輔

Fujiwara Kintō　藤原公任

Fujiwara Kiyosuke　藤原清輔

Fujiwara Kusuko　藤原薬子

Fujiwara Michinaga　藤原道長

Fujiwara Morosuke　藤原師輔

Fujiwara Mototoshi　藤原基俊

Fujiwara no Kachion　藤原勝臣

Fujiwara Norikane　藤原範兼

Fujiwara Okikaze　藤原興風

Fujiwara Shunzei　藤原俊成

Fujiwara Tadanobu 藤原斎信

Fujiwara Tameie 藤原為家

Fujiwara Yukinari 藤原行成

fukuro toji 袋綴

futai no nenbutsu
　ふたいの念仏（不退の念仏）

Genji monogatari 源氏物語

Genshin 源信

getsurinkan (gachirinkan) 月輪観

gō 業

Goichijō 後一条

gokuraku 極楽

Gosen wakashū 後撰和歌集

goshō 五障

Goshūi wakashū 後拾遺和歌集

Gosuzaku 後朱雀

Gyōki 行基

gyokinki 御禁忌

Gyokuyō wakashū 玉葉和歌集

Hachidaishū shō 八大集抄

Hakkō[e] 八講［会］

hanka 反歌

Hannya shingyō 般若心経

Harima 播磨

Hashimoto Yuri 橋本ゆり

Heizei 平城

Henjō 遍昭

Hie 比叡

higan 彼岸

Higashi Sanjōin 東三条院

Hikaru Genji 光源氏

Hitomaro [Kakinomoto Hitomaro]
　［柿本］人麿

hōchi 法池

Hokekyō 法華経

Hokke sanbukyō 法華三部経

hōmochi 法物

honji 本地

Hosshin wakashū 発心和歌集

Hosshin wakashū no kenkyū
　発心和歌集の研究

hotaru awase 螢合

hotoke　仏

hotsu bodaishin　発菩提心

Hou Han shu　後漢書

Hui-jian　慧簡

Ichijō　一条

Ichijō ōji　一条大路

imikotoba, imu　忌詞, 忌む

Ise　伊勢

Ise monogatari　伊勢物語

Ishihara Kiyoshi　石原清志

Issai nyorai kongō jumyō daranikyō
一切如来金剛壽命陀羅尼経

itsubon　乙本

Itsuki no miya　斎院, いつきのみや

itsutsu no sawari　五つの障り

Iwami no jo shiki　石見女式；
　Iwami no jo zuinō　石見女髄脳

Izumi Shikibu　和泉式部

Izumi Shikibu shū　和泉式部集

Izumo　出雲

jikkai　十戒

Jinkaku　深覚

jo　序

Jōfugyō bosatsu　常不軽菩薩

Jōgū Shōtoku Hōōtei setsu
上宮聖徳法王帝説

Jōgū Taishi den hoketsuki
上宮太子傳補闕記

Jōjin Ajari no haha shū
成尋阿闍梨母集

Jōtōmon'in　上東門院

Jūdaigan　十大願

jukkai　述懐

kago　歌語

Kakaishō　河海抄

Kakuchō　覺超

kami　神

Kamigamo Jinja　上賀茂神社

kaminaga　髪長

Kamo　賀茂

Kamo chūshin zakki　賀茂注進雑記

Kamo Daimyōjin　賀茂大明神

Kamo Jingūji　賀茂神宮寺

Kamo Kōtaijingū ki
　賀茂皇太神宮記

Kamo Mioya Jinja　賀茂御組神社

Kamo no Yasunori nyo shū
　賀茂保憲女集

Kamo Saiin ki　賀茂斎院記

Kamo Taketsunumi no mikoto
　賀茂建角身命

Kamo Wake Ikazuchi Jinja
　賀茂別雷神社

Kamo Wake Ikazuchi no mikoto
　賀茂別雷命

kana　仮名

Kanfugen bosatsu gyōbōgyō
　観普賢菩薩行法経

Kanfugengyō　観普賢経

Kangakue　勧学会

Kangen [era]　寛元

kanji　漢字

*Kanjizai Bosatsu nyoishin darani
　jukyō*
　観自在菩薩如意心陀羅尼呪経

Kankō [era]　寛弘

Kannon　観音

kannushi　神主

Kanpaku　関白

kanshi　漢詩

Kanzeon bosatsu fumon bon
　観世音菩薩普門品

Karasaki　唐崎

Kataoka[yama]　片岡[山]

Kazan　花山

kechien　結縁

Kegongyō　華厳経

Keiso (Kyōso)　慶祚

Kianmon'in　徽安門院

Kinbusen　金峰山

Ki no Tomonori　紀友則

Ki no Tsurayuki　紀貫之

kinsei　近世

Kin'yō wakashū　金葉和歌集

Kitamura Kigin　北村季吟

kō　劫

kōbon　甲本

Kōgon　光厳

Kohon setsuwa shū　古本説話集

Kojidan　古事談

Kojiki　古事記

Kokin wakashū　古今和歌集

kokoro　心

Konjaku monogatari shū
今昔物語集

Korai fūteishō　古来風体抄

Kōshin　庚申

kotobagaki　詞書

kudai　句題

Kudai waka　句題和歌

Kunaichō　宮内庁

Kuroda Toshio　黒田俊夫

kyōgen kigo　狂言綺語

Liu-Sung　劔末

makewaza mushi awase
負態虫合

makurakotoba　枕詞

Makura no sōshi　枕冊子

manajo　真名序

Man'yōshū　万葉集

Mara　摩羅

masugata retchōsō　枡形列帖装

Matsudaira Bunko　松平文庫

mekaminaga　女かみなが

Midō kanpaku ki　御堂関白記

Miidera　三井寺

mikkyō　密教

Minamoto Akikane　源顕兼

Minamoto Tamenori　源為憲

Minamoto Toshikata　源俊賢

Minamoto Toshiyori (Shunrai)
源俊頼

Minamoto Tsuneyori　源経頼

Miroku geshōkyō　弥勒下生経

Miroku jōshōkyō　弥勒上生経

Mitarashigawa　御手洗川

Monjushiri hotsugangyō
文殊師利発願経

mono awase　物合

monogatari　物語

Motoori Norinaga　本居宣長

Mujū Ichien　無住一円

Munehira　致平

Murakami　村上

Murasakino　紫野

Murasaki Shikibu　紫式部

Muromachi　室町

Muryōgikyō　無量義経

Muryōjukyō　無量壽経

Musashi　武蔵

Myōshōgon hon　妙荘厳品

Myōshōgon'ō honji hon
　妙荘厳王本事品

nenbutsu　念仏

Nihon kiryaku　日本紀略

Nihon ryōiki　日本靈異記

nijūhappon no uta
　二十八品の歌

nijūnisha　二十二社

nikki　日記

Nin'an [era]　仁安

Ninkō Shōnin　人康上人

Ninnō hannya haramitsugyō
　仁王般若波羅蜜経

nori ("Dharma") 法：
　noru ("ride on a vehicle") 乗る

Nyoirin daranikyō
　如意輪陀羅尼経

Ōe Chisato　大江千里

Ōgishō　奥義抄

ōjō　往生

Ōkagami　大鏡

Okamoto Yasuyoshi　岡本保可

okugaki　奥書

Onjōji　園城寺

Onna bettō　女別当

Onshi　婉子

rakushoku　落飾

Reigen　霊元

Reizei　令泉

rekishi-monogatari   歴史物語

Renjō   蓮上

rentaikei   連体形

rokkon   六根

rokujin   六塵

Saga   嵯峨

sai (toki)   斎

Saigū   斎宮

Saigyō   西行

Saiin   斎院

Saiin bettō   斎院別当

Sakeiki   左経記

sanbō   三宝

Sanbōe   三宝絵

Sanjō   三条

sanjūshichi dōbon   三十七道品

Sankashū   山家集

Sei Shōnagon   清少納言

Senshi (Higashi Sanjōin)   銓子

Senshi Naishinnō   選子内親王

Senzai wakashū   千歳和歌集

setai   世諦

setsuwa   説話

Shakkyōka   釈教歌

Shasekishū   沙石集

shi   詩

shibyō   四病

Shichishō nyoirin himitsu yōkyō   七星如意輪祕密要経

Shiguzeigan   四弘誓願

shikan   止観

shikashū   私歌集

Shika wakashū   詞花和歌集

shikishima no michi   敷きしまの道

Shimabara Shiritsu Kōminkan   島原市立公民館

Shimogamo Jinja   下賀茂神社

Shin chokusen wakashū   新勅撰和歌集

Shingyō   心経

Shin kokin wakashū   新古今和歌集

Shinpen kokka taikan   新編国歌大観

Shin senzai wakashū 新千歳和歌集

shintai 真諦

Shintō 神道

Shishi Naishinnō 資子内親王

Shō Kannon 正観音

Shōkū 性空

Shoku gosen wakashū
続後撰和歌集

Shoku goshūi wakashū
続後拾遺和歌集

Shoku senzai wakashū
続千歳和歌集

Shoku shūi wakashū 続拾遺和歌集

Shoryōbu 書陵部

Shosha [Mount] 書写[山]

Shōshi 彰子

Shōtoku [Prince, i.e. Shōtoku Taishi] 聖徳太子

Shōtoku Taishi denryaku
聖徳太子伝略

Shūi wakashū 拾遺和歌集

shukke 出家

shūshikei 終止形

somegami 染紙

Sonshi [Naishinnō] 尊子[内親王]

Sosei 素性

*Sui T'ien-t'ai Zhi-she Da-shi
bie-chuan* 隋天台智者大師別伝

Susa-no-o [no mikoto] 素戔鳴尊
(also 須佐之男命)

Suzaku 朱雀

Tahō nyorai 多宝如来

Taishaku 帝釋

Tamakatsuma 玉かつま

Tamayorihime no mikoto
玉依姫命

Tanao [Shrine] 棚尾

tanka 短歌

tendoku 転読

Ten'en [era] 天延

Tennyojōbutsukyō 転女成仏経

Tennyoshingyō 転女心経

Tenrinnō 天輪王

tō 塔

Tō [Fuji] Dainagon   藤大納言

Toshiyori zuinō   俊頼髄脳

Uchiko Naishinnō   有智子内親王

ubasoku   優婆塞

Urin'in   宇林院

utaawase   歌合

utakotoba   歌詞

waka   和歌

waka no michi   和歌之道

Wakan rōeishū   和漢朗詠集

waka soku darani   和歌即陀羅尼

Xiang-shan (monastery)   香山寺

Xuan-zang   玄奘

Yakuō bosatsu honji hon
薬王菩薩本事品

Yakushi rurikō kyō   薬師瑠璃光経

*Yakushi rurikō nyorai hongan
kudoku kyō*
薬師瑠璃光如来本願功徳経

Yamato monogatari   大和物語

yamato toji   大和綴

yamazato   山里

Yi-jing   義淨

yomu   詠む

Yoshino   吉野

Yotsutsuji Yoshinari   四辻善成

Yūgao   夕顔

Zhih-yi   智顗

Zhuang-zhi (Qiu-shui)   荘子（秋水）

Zuigan Yakushi kyō   隨願薬子経

BIBLIOGRAPHY

Abe Akio, Akiyama Ken, and Imai Gen'ei, eds. *Genji monogatari.* 6 vols. (*Nihon koten bungaku zenshū* 12–17). Tokyo: Shōgakukan, 1970–76.

Akiba Yasutarō, Suzuki Tomotarō, and Kishigami Shinji. "*Daisaiin saki no gyoshū no kenkyū.*" In *Nihon Daigaku sōritsu shichijūnen kinen ronbunshū*, vol. 1, *Jinbun kagaku hen*, 423–579. Tokyo: Nihon Daigaku, 1960.

Andō Masatsugu. "Imyō ingo no kenkyū o nobete, toku ni Saigū imikotoba o ronzu." In *Andō Masatsugu chosakushū*, vol. 5, *Nihon bunkashi ronkō*, 332–65. Tokyo: Yūsankaku, 1974.

Bowring, Richard, trans. *Murasaki Shikibu: Her Diary and Poetic Memoirs.* Princeton: Princeton University Press, 1982.

Conze, Edward, trans. *Buddhist Wisdom Books.* New York: Harper and Row/Harper Torchbooks, 1958.

Cranston, Edwin A. "The Dark Path: Images of Longing in Japanese Love Poetry." *Harvard Journal of Asiatic Studies* 35 (1975): 60–99.

Fujii Chikai. *Ōjōyōshū no bunkashiteki kenkyū.* Kyoto: Heiraku Shoten, 1978.

Grapard, Allan G. "Institution, Ritual and Ideology: The Twenty-Two Shrine-Temple Multiplexes of Heian Japan." *History of Religions* 27.3 (February 1988): 246–69.

———. "Japan's Ignored Cultural Revolution: The Separation of Shintō and Buddhist Divinities in Meiji (*shimbutsu bunri*) and a Case Study: Tōnomine." *History of Religions* 23.3 (February 1984): 240–65.

Groner, Paul. "*The Lotus Sutra* and Saichō's Interpretation of the Realization of Buddhahood with This Very Body." In *The Lotus Sutra in Japanese Culture*, edited by George J. Tanabe, Jr., and Willa Jane Tanabe, 95–117. Honolulu: University of Hawaii Press, 1989.

Hagitani Boku, ed. *Heianchō utaawase taisei.* 10 vols. Kyoto: Dōmeisha, reprinted 1979.

Hanawa Hokiichi, ed. *Gunsho ruijū.* 19 vols. Tokyo: Keizai Zasshisha, 1898–1902.

Hashimoto Fumio. *Ōchō waka shi no kenkyū.* Tokyo: Kasama Shoin, 1972.

———, Ariyoshi Tamotsu, and Fujihira Haruo, eds. *Karonshū* (*Nihon koten bungaku zenshū* 50). Tokyo: Shōgakukan, 1975.

Hurvitz, Leon, trans. *Scripture of the Lotus Blossom of the Fine Dharma.* New York and London: Columbia University Press, 1976.

Ichikawa Kansai, ed. *Nihon shiki.* Tokyo: Kokusho Kankōkai, 1911.

Idumi, H. [Izumi Hōkei]. "The Hymn on the Life and Vows of Samantabhadra, with the Sanskrit Text: *Bhadracarīpraṇidhāna.*" *The Eastern Buddhist* 5.2–3 (April 1930): 226–47.

Ishihara Kiyoshi. *Hosshin wakashū no kenkyū.* Osaka: Izumi Shoin, 1983.

———. *Shakkyōka no kenkyū.* Kyoto: Dōmeisha, 1980.

Itō Setsuko. "The Muse in Competition: *Uta-awase* Through the Ages." *Monumenta Nipponica* 37.2: 201–22.

Iwamoto Yutaka. *Daijō kyōten* 3 (*Bukkyō seiten sen* 5). Tokyo: Yomiuri Shinbunsha, 1976.

Kagawa Yoshio. "Bukkyō no joseikan." *Indogaku Bukkyōgaku kenkyū* 23.2 (March 1975): 45–52.

Kakimura Shigematsu, ed. *Honchō monzui chūshaku.* 2 vols. Tokyo: Fūzanbō, 1922, reprinted 1968.

Kamens, Edward. *The Three Jewels: A Study and Translation of Minamoto Tamenori's Sanbōe* (Michigan Monograph Series in Japanese Studies, Number 2). Ann Arbor: Center for Japanese Studies, The University of Michigan, 1988.

Kasahara Kazuo. *Nyonin ōjō shisō no keifu.* Tokyo: Yoshikawa Kōbunkan, 1975.

Katagiri Yōichi. *Utamakura utakotoba jiten* (*Kadokawa Shojiten* 35). Tokyo: Kadokawa Shoten, 1983.

Kawade Kiyohiko. "Saiinnai no seikatsu o shinobu." *Shintō shi kenkyū* 16.1 (1968): 26–46.

Kawaguchi Hisao, ed. *Kohon setsuwa shū* (*Nihon koten zensho*). Tokyo: Asahi Shinbunsha, 1967.

Kikuchi Hitoshi. "Waka darani kō." *Denshō bungaku kenkyū* 27 (January 1983): 1–12.

Koizumi Hiroshi and Takahashi Nobuyuki, eds. *Shohon taishō Sanbōe shūsei.* Tokyo: Kasama Shoin, 1980.

Kokushi daijiten Henshū Iinkai, ed. *Kokushi daijiten.* Tokyo: Yoshikawa Kōbunkan, 1979–.

Kokusho Kankōkai, ed. *Zoku zoku gunsho ruijū.* 16 vols. Tokyo: Kokusho Kankōkai, 1906–9.

Kubo Noritada. *Kōshin shinkō.* Tokyo: Yamakawa Shuppansha, 1956, reprinted 1971.

Kuroda Toshio. "Shintō in the History of Japanese Religion." *The Journal of Japanese Studies* 7.1 (Winter 1981): 1–21. (Translated by James C. Dobbins and Suzanne Gay.)

Kuroita Katsumi, ed. *[Shintei zōho] Kokushi taikei.* 38 vols. Tokyo: *Kokushi taikei* Kankōkai, 1929–62.

McCullough, Helen Craig. *Brocade by Night: Kokin wakashū and the Court Style in Japanese Court Poetry.* Stanford: Stanford University Press, 1985.

———, trans. *Ōkagami, the Great Mirror: Fujiwara Michinaga (966–1027) and His Times.* Princeton: Princeton University Press, and Tokyo: University of Tokyo Press, 1980.

McCullough, William and Helen Craig McCullough, trans. *A Tale of Flowering Fortunes: Annals of Japanese Aristocratic Life in the Heian Period.* 2 vols. Stanford: Stanford University Press, 1980.

McMullin, Neil. "Historical and Historiographical Issues in the Study of Pre-Modern Japanese Religion." *Japanese Journal of Religious Studies* 16.1 (March 1989): 3–40.

Mekada Sakuo. *"Hosshin wakashū* to Daisaiin Senshi." In *Bukkyō bungaku kenkyū*, series 2 no. 1, edited by Bukkyō Bungaku Kenkyūkai, 9–26. Kyoto: Hōzōkan, 1974.

Miller, Roy Andrew. "No Time for Literature." *Journal of the American Oriental Society* 107.4 (October-December 1987): 745–60.

Minegishi Yoshiaki. *Heian jidai waka bungaku no kenkyū.* Tokyo: Ōfūsha, 1966.

———— and Momota Michio. *Tōzai joryū bungei saron: Chūgū Teishi to Danbuiei Kōshaku Fujin.* Tokyo: Kasama Shoin, 1978.

Mochizuki Shinkō. *Bukkyō daijiten.* 10 vols. Rev. ed. Tokyo: Sekai Seiten Kankō Kyōkai, 1958–63.

Morrell, Robert E. "The Buddhist Poetry in the *Goshūishū.*" *Monumenta Nipponica* 28.1 (Spring 1973): 87–138.

————, trans. *Sand and Pebbles: The Tales of Mujū Ichien, A Voice for Pluralism in Kamakura Buddhism.* Albany: State University of New York Press, 1985.

Motofusa Naoko. "Daisaiin saron no kashū ni okeru *Kokinshū* no eikyō." *Heian bungaku kenkyū* 64 (December 1980): 45–66.

Muromatsu Iwao, ed. *Kokubun chūshaku zensho.* 20 vols. Tokyo: Kokugakuin Daigaku Shuppanbu, 1907–10.

Naka Shūko. "Josei saron ni okeru shizen to waka: Daisaiin saron o chūshin ni." In *Ōchō waka no sekai: shizen kanjō to biishiki*, edited by Katagiri Yōichi, 60–75. Tokyo: Sekai Shisōsha, 1984.

Nihon koten bungaku taikei (NKBT). 100 vols. Tokyo: Iwanami Shoten, 1957–69.

Oguri Junko. *Nyonin ōjō: Nihon shi ni okeru onna no sukui.* Tokyo: Jinbun Shoin, 1987.

Okazaki Tomoko. *Heian joryū sakka no kenkyū.* Kyoto: Hōzōkan, 1967.

————. "Shakkyōka kō: hachidaishū o chūshin ni." In *Bukkyō bungaku kenkyū* 1, edited by Bukkyō Bungaku Kenkyūkai, 79–118. Kyoto: Hōzōkan, 1963.

Ozawa Masao. *Kokinshū no sekai.* Tokyo: Hanawa Shobō, 1961.

————. "Kudai shi to kudai waka." *Kokugo to kokubungaku* 29.11 (November 1952): 9–20.

Paul, Diana Y. *Women in Buddhism: Images of the Feminine in the Mahāyāna Tradition.* 2d ed. Berkeley: University of California Press, 1985.

Paz, Octavio. *Sor Juana, or The Traps of Faith.* Cambridge: The Belknap Press of Harvard University Press, 1988.

Sakamoto Yukio and Iwamoto Yutaka, eds. and trans. *Hokekyō.* 3 vols. (*Iwanami Bunko* 33–304–1, 2, and 3). Tokyo: Iwanami Shoten, 1962–67.

Sasaki Nobutsuna, ed. *Nihon kagaku taikei.* 10 vols. Tokyo: Kazama Shobō, 1956–63.

Sasaki Takiko. "Daisaiin Senshi Naishinnō no waka." In *Chūsei setsuwa no sekai*, edited by Hokkaidō Daigaku Setsuwa Bungaku Kenkyūkai, 231–56. Tokyo: Kasama Shoin, 1979.

Shinpen kokka taikan Henshū Iinkai, ed. *Shinpen kokka taikan (SKT).* Tokyo: Kadokawa Shoten, 1983–.

Suzuki Hideo. "*Kokinshū*-teki hyōgen no keisei." *Bungaku* 42.5 (May 1974): 63–77.

Takagi Yutaka. *Heian jidai hokke bukkyō shi no kenkyū*. Kyoto: Heirakuji Shoten, 1973.

Takakusu Junjirō and Watanabe Kaigyoku, eds. *Taishō shinshū daizōkyō*. 85 vols. Tokyo: Taishō Issaikyō Kankōkai, 1924–32.

Takamine Ryōshū. *Kegon ronshū*. Tokyo: Kokusho Kankōkai, 1976.

Tanaka Kōichi. "Daisaiin Senshi no shinkō seikatsu to *Hosshin wakashū* no seiritsu." *Kokubungaku kō* 71 (August 1976): 12–21.

Taya Raishun, Ochō E'nichi, and Funahashi Issai, eds. *Bukkyōgaku jiten*. Kyoto: Hōzōkan, 1955.

Tokiwa Daijō et al., eds. *Shakkyō kaei zenshū*. 6 vols. 1936, reprinted Osaka: Tōhō Shuppan, 1978.

Tokoro Kyōko. "Senshi Naishinnō Saiin kankei no wakashūsei." *Shintō shi kenkyū* 35.2 (April 1987): 61–83.

———. "Saiin Senshi Naishinnō no Bukkyō shinkō." *Shintō shi kenkyū* 32.3 (July 1984): 21–60.

———. "Senshi Naishinnō nenpu kō." *Kodai bunka* 36.4 (April 1984): 28–41.

Tōkyō Daigaku Shiryō Hensan Sho, ed. *Midō kanpaku ki (Dai Nihon kokiroku)*. 3 vols. Tokyo: Iwanami Shoten, 1952–54.

Waka Shi Kenkyūkai, ed. *Shikashū taisei*. 7 vols. Tokyo: Meiji Shoin, 1973–76.

Washio Junkei et al., eds. *Kokubun Tōhō Bukkyō sōsho*. 10 vols. Tokyo: Tōhō Shoin, 1925.

Watson, Burton, trans. *Japanese Literature in Chinese*, vol. 1, *Poetry and Prose by Japanese Writers of the Early Period*. New York and London: Columbia University Press, 1975.

Yamada Shōzen. "Poetry and Meaning: Medieval Poets and the *Lotus Sūtra*." In *The Lotus Sutra in Japanese Culture*, edited by George J. Tanabe, Jr., and Willa Jane Tanabe, 95–117. Honolulu: University of Hawaii Press, 1989. (Translated by Willa Jane Tanabe.)

———. "Getsurinkan to chūsei waka." In *Katō Shōichi sensei koki kinen ronbunshū: Bukkyō to girei*, edited by Bukkyō Minzoku Gakkai, 301–14. Tokyo: Kokusho Kankōkai, 1977.

———. "Chūsei kōki ni okeru waka soku darani no jissen." *Indogaku Bukkyōgaku kenkyū* 16.1 (December 1967): 290–92.

Yamagishi Tokuhei, ed. *Hachidaishū zenchū*. 3 vols. Tokyo: Yūseidō, 1960.

Yamazato Keiseki. "Daisaiin Senshi Naishinnō no Bukkyō." *Ryūkoku shidan* 56–57 (December 1966): 373–400.

Yanai Shigeshi. "Kangakue ni okeru shakkyōshi." *Kyōritsu Daigaku Tanki Daigakubu kiyō* 7 (December 1963): 16–27.

Yoshikawa Kōjirō, Satake Akihiro, and Hino Tatsuo, eds. *Motoori Norinaga*. (*Nihon shisō taikei* 40). Tokyo: Iwanami Shoten, 1978.

Zōho shiryō taisei Kankōkai, ed. *Zōho shiryō taisei*. 45 vols. Kyoto: Rinsen Shoten, 1965.

INDEX

ABOUT THE AUTHOR

Edward Kamens is the author of *The Three Jewels: A Study and Translation of Minamoto Tamenori's Sanbōe* (Michigan Monograph Series in Japanese Studies, Number 2) and other studies of premodern Japanese prose and poetry. He is Assistant Professor in the Department of East Asian Languages and Literatures at Yale University.